Daylighting, Architecture and Health

Building Design Strategies

Daylighting, Architecture and Health

Building Design Strategies

Mohamed Boubekri

AMSTERDAM • BOSTON • HEIDELBERG • LONDON • NEW YORK • OXFORD
PARIS • SAN DIEGO • SAN FRANCISCO • SINGAPORE • SYDNEY • TOKYO
Architectural Press is an imprint of Elsevier

ELSEVIER

Architectural
Press

Architectural Press is an imprint of Elsevier
Linacre House, Jordan Hill, Oxford OX2 8DP, UK
30 Corporate Drive, Suite 400, Burlington, MA 01803, USA

First edition 2008

British Library Cataloguing in Publication Data
Boubekri, Mohamed
   Daylighting, architecture and health : building design strategies
   1. Daylighting 2. Architectural design — Health aspects 3. Light -
   Physiological effect I. Title
   729.2'8

Library of Congress Catalog Number: 2008928472

ISBN: 978-0-7506-6724-1

For information on all Architectural Press publications
visit our website at www.elsevierdirect.com

Typeset by CharonTec Ltd., A Macmillan Company.
(www.macmillansolutions.com)

Printed and bound in Great Britain by MPG Books Ltd

08 09 10 11   11 10 9 8 7 6 5 4 3 2 1

To my mother and to my late father
To Farah, Elyes and Yanis.

Contents

Acknowledgements

I wish to thank the many individuals who contributed so graciously towards the realization of this manuscript. First I'd like to thank my family for their love, sacrifice, moral support, patience and forgiveness. Many friends and colleagues have been more than generous in providing me with illustrations included in this book. Here I need to mention the eminent architect Tadao Ando, my friends and colleagues Jay Davidson, Scott Murphy and my former student Angel Valtiera. A very special mention of gratitude goes to my friend and colleague James Warfield who has provided me with many photographs for this book. I need to mention the extraordinary work of Audrey Hodgins whose professional contribution in the editing phase of the book was invaluable. I also can't overlook the help of two my graduate students, Mohamad Araji and Nora Wang who helped with many of graphics used in this book and I am very grateful for their help. Finally, this book would not have been possible without the financial support of the board of trustees of the University of Illinois at Urbana-Champaign.

Introduction

Without question, a causal relationship exists between the indoor environment and human health. The need for housing regulations and urban planning policies dates back to the mid-nineteenth century, when it became apparent that rampant diseases and epidemics in many cities of the newly industrialized world were caused partially by the physical ambient environment and were a problem to be dealt with. Deplorable sanitary conditions prevailed and were exacerbated by large migrations from villages to urban centers as rural residents sought work in factories. Links between man-made environments and epidemics such as tuberculosis have been historically recognized and largely overcome by planners and policy makers in the developed countries. Nevertheless, the effects of poorly designed buildings, whether in terms of limited access to sunlight or poor indoor air quality, continue to affect the health of building occupants. A 1998 World Health Organization report noted that up to 30% of new and remodeled buildings worldwide may be linked to health problems. 'Sick Building Syndrome' (SBS) is a term used to describe situations in which building occupants experience discomfort and even acute health problems that appear to be related to time spent in the building, even when no specific illness or cause can be identified. SBS is frequently associated with issues of indoor air quality; however, the contributing factors often relate to a combination of possible causes, including indoor air pollution, the absence of sunlight or daylight, inadequate heating or ventilation, poor acoustics, and the presence of asbestos. Biological contamination is also of concern. For example, lack of sunlight combined with high humidity can trigger the formation of mold and mildew spores, airborne contaminants that may lead to respiratory diseases. Some symptoms of SBS may be acute and easily treatable; others can be expressed in long-term, chronic ailments.

The relationship between the environment and health may not always be simple or direct (Lindheim, 1983). The assumption used to be that diseases were caused solely by a direct exposure to pathogenic viruses or microbes. More recently researchers have suggested that diseases are the result of a triangular relationship between the person, the pathogenic agent (virus or microbe), and the environment in which the person lives (Dubos, 1965; Cassel, 1976; Audy & Duan, 1974) (Figure 1). The physical, social, and economic environment can influence the level of resistance to a given pathogenic agent and, consequently, exacerbate or lessen health problems.

Daylight in general, and sunlight in particular, are vital to life on earth, and it is not difficult to believe that their absence fosters conditions that promote disease. Through photosynthesis and other processes, sunlight provides photochemical ingredients necessary for our lives. There are fundamental biological, hormonal, and physiological functions coordinated by cycles that are crucial to life for cells, plants, animals, and humans. Many plants and animals, including humans, develop abnormal behaviors and diseases when sunlight is absent because their diurnal cycle is disturbed.

If we are to function optimally, we need to be in tune with the natural environment into which humans came a few millennia ago. Sunlight serves as the link to the outside world when we are indoors, facilitating our essential connection with nature and giving us a sense of time and our position in that daily cycle. Buildings that we erect to shelter ourselves from the harsh environment create filters between us and nature. Yet we do not feel completely comfortable away from the natural environment, perhaps because the man-made environment is relatively young. As stated by Rudofsky (1964), '*To stave off physical and mental deterioration, the*

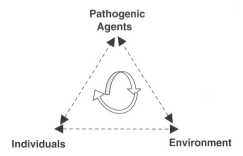

Figure 1   Triangular causal relationship of health causation model.

urban dweller periodically escapes his splendidly appointed lair to seek bliss in what he thinks are primitive surroundings: a cabin, a tent, or if he is less hidebound, a fishing village or hill town abroad.'

Increased urbanization since the turn of the twentieth century has led to the erection of concrete, glass, and steel skyscrapers (Figure 2). Tall buildings eclipse streets, limiting the movement of fresh air, eroding the immediate connection

Figure 2   Aerial view of New York City (courtesy of Dreamstime).

between ourselves and the natural environment. Modern socioeconomic forces require us to live and work in urban centers, and we often need to make a special trip, a separate experience from our daily lives, in order to come into contact with nature. In the United States, and indeed in many places around the world, urban centers abound where access to sunlight at street level is minimal if not nonexistent. Some downtown streets of American cities such as New York and Chicago receive little sunlight, yet people live and work there year round (Figure 3).

Over the last three or four decades, discussion about daylighting as a viable design option has been intimately linked to the debate about energy conservation in building design. The term 'daylighting' as used here is not the by-product of building fenestration but rather the active and controlled use of natural light for building illumination. Growing concerns about global warming, the ozone layer, depletion of fossil energy sources, and soaring oil prices have put energy efficiency at the vanguard of architectural research and practice. Statistics support the energy argument. According to the 1998 Energy Information Agency of the U.S. Department of Energy, the building sector is responsible for about 36% of all the energy consumed in the United States, more energy than the transportation sector (27%) and an amount almost equal to that used by the industrial sector (38%). Lighting is responsible for 30% to 50% of all the energy utilized in commercial and office buildings. Some surveys indicate

Figure 3   A New York city street on a clear sunny day (courtesy of Dreamstime).

even higher percentages. For commercial and office buildings occupied during the day studies have shown that total electricity and peak demand savings of 20–40% in lighting and cooling can be achieved with the proper use of daylight photosensors along with other energy-saving systems. Despite the potential for enormous energy savings of daylighting, efforts to curtail energy consumption have been primarily technologically driven, relying on improving the optical and energy efficiency of electric lighting, rather than using renewable sources of energy such as daylight. The use of renewable or low-energy sources is not yet a mainstream part of architectural practice. Daylighting standards should require a certain amount of daylight inside buildings for a certain duration. Despite incentive programs such as the Leadership in Energy and Environmental Design (LEED) of the U.S. Green Building Council, the Energy Star Program of the United States Environmental Protection Agency, and other programs worldwide, regulatory bodies have not successfully established compulsory daylighting standards (Boubekri, 2004a). One of the chief obstacles to instituting daylighting requirements in building codes has to do with the types of lighting standards that are currently practiced. These standards tend to be formulated either as energy consumption standards or in terms of light levels necessary for visual performance. There is an implicit understanding that the recommended levels for visual performance are intended to be average minimum levels. They are also meant for static illumination pertaining mostly to artificial light sources. As such, they do not explicitly relate to daylighting situations which are dynamic in nature, changing according to the time and the seasons, and cannot always be relied upon. Therefore, if daylighting standards were to be legislated, a minimum quantity of illuminance would need to be prescribed (as is the case in electric lighting standards) as well as a stipulation for the duration of these daylight levels.

There is an increasing interest in daylighting that moves beyond the traditional argument of energy conservation. Many experts realize that daylight affects people in a number of ways; it helps fulfill our psychological needs through inherent and unique qualities that are not easy to imitate artificially. Some of these functions are obvious but others are less so.

It is generally accepted that we feel better under daylight conditions. Many post-occupancy evaluations and surveys of office buildings indicate that workers prefer environments that have windows compared with those that don't. We feel energized, cheerful, and in a better mood when the sun is shining, but we feel grim, even depressed, during wintry or cloudy days. We often add skylights to our homes just to have more natural light. Daylighting apertures allow building occupants to connect with the outside world. Without this connection, we feel that something is missing. Michael Cohen, an educator who runs *Project NatureConnect* in Roche Harbor, Washington, an educational counseling service that uses applied ecopsychology and ecotherapy, reports that '*many such psychological problems as anxiety, chronic tension, and eating disorders are caused by our isolation from natural settings. We spend too much time indoors in artificial, man-made environments. It's unnatural and unhealthy.*' (Cohen, 1984). Our continuing efforts to 'connect' with the outside world are substantiated by numerous studies. Providing gardens and views through windows help hospital patients recover and heal faster than do patients who lack these amenities (Ulrich, 1984; Verderber, 1986; Verderber and Reuman, 1987). In 'Healing by design' Forman and colleagues (1996) wrote, '*Medical care cannot be separated from the buildings in which it is delivered. The quality of space in such buildings affects the outcome of medical care, and architectural design is thus an important part of the healing process.*'

Because of anecdotal and personal experience, architects assume that daylight (or sunlight) is healthier than artificial light. We may not yet know or understand all the causes of the 'feel good' or positive effects of natural light; yet, medical science has provided ample information on the positive effects of the causal relationships between light, good or bad, and certain physiological and psychological aspects of human health. Many cities have local zoning ordinances mandating public access to sunlight in the streets; however, sunlight (or daylight) for the most part is still considered an amenity in homes and workplaces. The salient question is whether it is really only an amenity or whether it is essential to our lives and welfare. A growing body of evidence suggests that the common thread that links several ailments is the absence of sunlight where we live and work. The scarcity of daylight causes some people to experience depression, dementia, disturbed circadian rhythm, bone frailty, renal dysfunction, weakened immune system, and other maladies, as will be shown in subsequent chapters. Links have been established between the scholastic achievements of schoolchildren and daylight in their classrooms; pupils who experience daylight in their schools tend to do significantly better than students who do not. Similar associations were found between performance in the workplace and daylighting. Although health and psychological benefits may become apparent only in the long term, they are nonetheless factual and should be taken into consideration. Some experts suggest that the case for daylighting would resonate more strongly if its health and psychological benefits were put at the forefront of the argument instead of, or in addition to, the advantages of energy savings.

Obviously, there is plenty of sunshine outdoors, if we can be outside for long enough periods. Studies suggest that we spend more than 80% of our lifetime indoors (Baker, 1998). Many segments of our population do not receive sunlight for prolonged periods of time for a number of reasons. There are those who are sick and bedridden and there are the elderly whose mobility depends on care providers and who may have less access to sunlight than younger populations. When it becomes difficult to move easily, access to sunlight loses priority even though its benefits can be crucial. Other sunlight-deficient populations include people who live in northern latitudes and who, in the winter, go to work long before the sun is up and return home when the sun has already set. There are also those who spend their entire working lives in windowless warehouses, factories, laboratories, or basements and receive no daylight for extended periods of time.

We also cannot simply assume that everybody has the time and the ability to get adequate exposure to sunlight through outdoor activities. Studies indicate that this can be a misconception, even in the warmest, most clement climates. A study in San Diego, California, measured the degree of exposure to the outdoors by an active adult population ranging in age between 40 and 64 years (Espiritu *et al.*, 1994). It found that people in this age group spent little time outdoors and certainly no more than other populations where the climate was less clement. The results of the San Diego study agreed with previous assertions that people are generally not exposed to adequate quantities of sunlight (Okudaira *et al.*, 1983; Savides *et al.*, 1986; Campbell *et al.*, 1988; Kriptke *et al.*, 1989). It is therefore imperative that buildings be designed to meet that need. It is not sufficient to rely on the mere presence of windows and to assume that daylight will be adequate. We need to address the question of how much exposure to sunlight or daylight is essential in our lives.

Designing with the sun:
A historical perspective

1

As a formal subject of architectural study, daylighting arguably originated in northern Europe in the late nineteenth and early twentieth centuries. However, in one way or another, we have made use of the sun since the beginning of man's existence. It is said that the history of architecture is the history of human beings coping with the elements, and different civilizations have applied solar principles according to their own environmental and geographical contexts and according to their own knowledge and belief systems. Primitive human beings were primarily concerned with food and shelter and the imperatives of climate. Caves were used as dwellings and provided protection from the enemy and the harsh weather. Our interface with the sun and the natural environment can be traced throughout history, sometimes on a mystical or religious level and sometimes more concretely in stone walls and built structures.

1.1 THE SUN GOD

The many points of light that fill the night sky have always mystified human beings, spurring feelings of wonder and reverence. For the Babylonians and many other civilizations, the symbol for God was a star, but the sun has been given special attention in most cultures. Examples abound throughout history.

In Ancient Egypt, the Divine Father was the sun god Ra, the supreme ruler of all creation. The ruling Pharaoh was his offspring and his representative on earth (Quirke, 2001). The ancient Egyptians believed that each night the sun god journeyed on an *evening barque* within the bowels of the earth to fight evil but emerged triumphantly every morning in the east bringing warmth and sunlight, a perpetual daily return to the sky that signified the triumph of life over death and good over evil.

The religious beliefs related to the sun influenced and informed the town planning and the architecture of ancient Egyptian cities. The Pharaonic city of *Iunu,* referred to by the Greeks as Heliopolis or 'the city of the sun,' represented the geographical center of the sun cult that existed in ancient Egypt. Little is known today about this city, but its relative importance appears to have been highly significant to that civilization. Its name appears in Pharaonic religious literature more frequently than that of any other ancient Egyptian city. What is known is that the Pharaohs applied astronomic principles with extreme accuracy and rigor in temple building and perhaps other forms of habitation. The layouts of Egyptian temples such as Karnak were usually informed by the movements of the sun and accommodated seasonal variations (Figures 1.1, 1.2 and 1.3).

Located on the east bank of the Nile in Thebes, Egypt, Karnak is known as the solstice solar temple. Many of its features were built along an east–west axis that acknowledged the movement of the sun and a north–south line that mirrored ancient Egypt's geographic shape and the course of the Nile. In addition, Karnak had special alignments that corresponded to the summer and winter solstices. The winter solstice sunrise appears in the east in the archway of the axis of Karnak celebrating the sun god Ra through its majestic pillars (Figures 1.2 and 1.3).

The belief that the sun was the supreme creator of the universe was not unique to the ancient Egyptians. Ancient sites worldwide have been attuned to the annual journey of the sun across the sky. In Mayan mythology, the sun god created the first Inca, Manco Paca, and his sister on the Isle of the Sun in Lake Titicaca. He then instructed the two of them to set out and teach the civilized way of living to the other Indians who were living in 'darkness and ignorance.' The Incas celebrated the summer solstice with solemnity

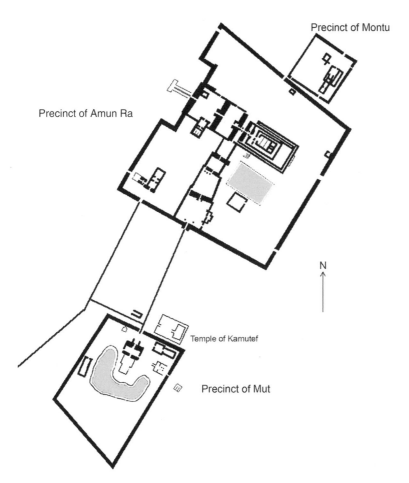

Precinct of Montu

Precinct of Amun Ra

N

Temple of Kamutef

Precinct of Mut

Figure 1.1   Plan of Karnak Temple laid out with winter and summer solstices in mind such that the winter solstice sunrise appears in the archway of the main axis of the temple (graphics by Charles Miller).

and reverence and made the most of the power of the sun in their architecture. They laid out the city of Machu Picchu (Figure 1.4), sometimes called the 'lost city of the Incas,' at 2430 m above sea level with its walls primarily facing east and south to capture and store the heat. Because wood and combustible fuels were difficult to obtain at high altitudes, they were replaced by passive solar heating. Located in the sacred and primary zone of the three main sectors of the city of Machu Picchu, the Temple of the Sun (Figure 1.5), known as the Intihuatana, was dedicated to the most revered and greatest deity, the sun god.

Figure 1.2   The main axis of the temple Karnak with the hypostyle hall at midpoint along the axis (photo by Dreamstime).

1.2   SUNLIGHT INFORMING CAVE AND UNDERGROUND ARCHITECTURE

Sunlight has warmed the caves that have provided human habitat since our original ancestors first sought shelter, more than a million years ago, and has remained a primary factor

Figure 1.3   The sun striking pillars along the main axis of Karnak temple (courtesy of Dreamstime).

in the design of habitations. Examples abound of our innate understanding of the importance of the sun in our dwellings. Whether it was the troglodytic towns such as those in Matmata, Tunisia (Figure 1.6) or in Xian, China (Figure 1.7), the underground cave communities that punctuated the hills of Cappadocia in Turkey (Figures 1.8 and 1.9), the hills of the Spanish town of Guadix in the province of Granada that dates from Phoenician and Roman times and that can be seen from the outside only through its dazzling whitewashed chimneys and doorways punctuating the hills (Figure 1.10), the cliff dwellings in the Dogon territory in Mali (Figure 1.11),

Figure 1.4   Machu Picchu, with building walls primarily facing east and south to capture and store the heat (courtesy of James P. Warfield).

the whitewashed houses hanging on the hills of the Greek island of Santorini (Figure 1.12), or the cave temples of the Yungang Grottos built by Buddhist missionaries in Datong in the province of Shanxi in China (Figure 1.13), people have not only carved architecture in accordance with their needs to survive wars and predators but also to be in harmony with the environment in which they lived. Their awareness of the bounties of the sun was omnipresent. They selected sites for their habitat and places of worship, shaped their dwellings and carved openings within their walls and sunken court-yards to optimize solar exposure and provide heat, cool and shade, and protection from the enemy. For many of these communities, the sun was the primary source of heating and an essential source of comfort and well-being.

Native populations of the American southwest exhibited similar sensitivity towards the sun, as did other indigenous cultures. This sensitivity can be seen in their cliff dwellings and pueblos. Native American mythology was interwoven with nature, especially with the sun's numinous powers and its benevolent and therapeutic qualities. The cliff dwellings of the Ancestral Pueblo Indians demonstrate such an understanding. Perched high on cliffs among massive canyons, the location of these caves discouraged predators and ensured exposure to sunlight: two essential criteria for the habitations of American Indians. In the protected niches and alcoves of the canyons of Utah, Arizona, and New Mexico from approximately AD 600 to AD 1200, the cliff pueblos were an elaborate complex

Figure 1.5 Intihuatana, the temple of the sun dedicated to the sun god in the sacred district of the city of Machu Picchu (courtesy of Dreamstime).

of multistoried buildings assembled in terraced and set back formations that opened to the sky and the sunlight for winter heating, while the upper edges of the towering cliffs provided shade during the hot summer (Figures 1.14, 1.15 and 1.16).

1.3 SUN-INFORMED ARCHITECTURE OF CLASSICAL GREECE

In other times and other parts of the world, a similar understanding of the benefits of the natural environment can be

Figure 1.6 Troglodytic town of Matmata, Tunisia (courtesy of James P. Warfield).

found, including in ancient Greek architecture. The classical Greek period extends from the Battle of Marathon in 490 BC to the Hellenistic age, which extends to the year 30 BC. Like many preceding civilizations, classical Greece expressed a reverence for the sun and its numinous powers, a characteristic visible in the architecture of places of worship and Greek dwellings. Following the design of Egyptian temples, the ancient Greeks typically oriented the front façade of their temples eastward. Important religious ceremonies took place in the eastern section of the temple, which was illuminated by the early morning rays of the sun (Figure 1.17).

Solar design principles transcended the symbolic reverence for the sun found in the religious buildings of classical Greece. It was a useful, perhaps even necessary commodity that provided a source of warmth in domestic architecture. A dialogue between light and shadows appeared as a fundamental design element of the Greek vernacular architecture. Buildings were built with thick walls that transferred the solar heat of winter or the coolness of the summer night into the interior, while deep whitewashed wall apertures ushered light into the space. In 400 BC Socrates, who apparently lived in a solar-heated house, wrote about the sun, outlining some basic design principles. In his book, *Xenophon's Memorabilia*, he observed as follows (Strauss, 1972):

Now in houses with a south aspect, the sun's rays penetrate into the porticos in winter, but in the summer,

Figure 1.7 Underground dwelling in Xian, China (courtesy of James P. Warfield).

the path of the sun is right over our heads and above the roof, so that there is shade. If then this is the best arrangement, we should build the south side loftier to get the winter sun and the north side lower to keep out the winter winds. To put it shortly, the house in which the owner can find a pleasant retreat at all seasons and can store his belongings safely is presumably at once the pleasantest and the most beautiful.

Figure 1.8   Underground dwellings in Cappadocia, Turkey, Asia Minor (courtesy of James P. Warfield).

Figure 1.9   Underground dwellings in Cappadocia, Turkey, Asia Minor (courtesy of James P. Warfield).

The Greeks believed in democratizing solar access, as was apparent in the town planning of model communities such as Olynthus and Priene. Built in the fourth century AD, Priene was one of these solar cities attesting to the Greeks' genuine appreciation of the goodness and power of the sun. This newly developed settlement on Mount Mycale was built by residents who relocated their homes to escape frequent

Figure 1.10 Underground dwelling in the City of Guadix, Spain (courtesy of James P. Warfield).

Figure 1.11 Cliff granaries of Teli in the Dogon territory in Mali (courtesy of James P. Warfield).

floods (Butti and Perlin, 1980). One solar design feature was a checkerboard street grid facing east–west and north–south. Another was the south-facing hill on which the town was laid out to take maximum advantage of the sun.

Solar architectural design in ancient Greece was neither a novelty nor a symbol of economic status of the builder.

Figure 1.12   Whitewashed cliff dwellings in Santorini, Greece (courtesy of James P. Warfield).

Leading archeologists, including J. Walter Graham (1972), agree that access to sunlight was a practical preoccupation that cut across economic and social strata. The sun was plentiful, wood was scarce, and rich and poor alike relied on the sun to heat their homes. A typical house had a southern section, occupied mostly in the winter, and a northern one to be used during the hot summer months. The southern portion would

Figure 1.13 Buddhist cave temple in the in Datong, Shanxi, China (courtesy of James P. Warfield).

Figure 1.14 The 800-year-old Indian cliff dwellings of Mesa Verde, Colorado (courtesy of James P. Warfield).

be lower than the northern section to allow the sun into the inner part of the centrally located courtyard (Figure 1.18).

Besides being a source of heat, the Greeks believed the sun fostered good health. The playwright Aeschylus believed that only 'barbarians' and 'primitives' lived in caves and places devoid of sunlight. In *Promethius Bound*, he wrote:

Though they had eyes to see, they saw to no avail; they had ears, but understood not ... They lacked knowledge

Figure 1.15 Terraced Indian dwellings at Mesa Verde, Colorado (courtesy of James P. Warfield).

of houses turned to face the winter sun, dwelling beneath the ground like swarming ants in sunless caves. (Butti and Perlin, 1980)

Oribasius, an eminent medical writer and the personal physician of Julian the Apostate, wrote in the fourth century AD that the least healthy side of a building was the northern one because '*it doesn't receive any sunlight most of the time and when it does, the sun rays falls obliquely and without much vitality.*' The southern façade was deemed to be the healthy side (Grant and Oribasius, 1997).

1.4 SUNLIGHT IN THE ARCHITECTURE OF CLASSICAL ROME

Roman civilization is often grouped into 'classical antiquity' with ancient Greece, a civilization that inspired much of the culture of ancient Rome, and we should not be surprised to discover that, when it comes to solar design principles, the Romans applied them just as the Greeks had done. The writings of Vitruvius, the eminent Roman architect in the first century BC, influenced architects for centuries to come, including Palladio from the Rennaissance period and up to and including the modern age. In Vitruvius's *Ten Books of Architecture* (Morgan, 1914), he wrote: '*Buildings should be thoroughly shut in rather than exposed toward the north, and*

Figure 1.16   White House, Canyon de Chelley, New Mexico (courtesy of James P. Warfield).

the main portion should face the warmer south side.' Many Roman houses featured a solar furnace known as 'heliocaminus' in their design. Much like the modern sunspace in a passive solar strategy, the heliocaminus was a separate space within the house where solar heat could be trapped and then distributed to other quarters of the house as needed. The Pantheon of Rome, one of the most famous Roman temples

Figure 1.17   The early morning sun striking the main portal of the Athena Nike temple at the Acropolis, Greece (courtesy of Dreamstime).

which was destroyed along with other buildings in a huge fire in AD 80, was later rebuilt by the emperor Hadrian between AD 118 and AD 125, incorporating solar heating principles. The oculus on top of the dome of the main rotunda captures the zenithal sunbeams that heat and illuminate the rotunda, and

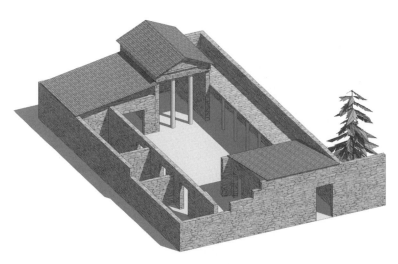

Figure 1.18 Typical Greek house with the southern section lower than the northern section to allow the sunlight in during winter (courtesy of Mohamad Araji).

epitomizes the Romans' awareness of the importance of sunlight in their architecture (Figure 1.19).

The Romans are known to have pioneered the technology of glass window coverings, which they used to capture and trap solar heat to warm their homes, their baths, and their greenhouses where they cultivated plants, flowers, fruits, and vegetables. Plants would then grow more quickly to produce fruits and vegetables all year round. Although glass had been used for nearly 3000 years by other civilizations in the Middle East and Africa, its use as a window to admit light and prevent rain and cold from entering a building was said to be a Roman creation.

Not only did the Romans use solar energy to heat small homes, but they also relied on it to partly heat large public buildings (Tatcher, 1956; Ring, 1996), such as the public baths of Ostia and Caracalla (Figure 1.20).

The Romans also pioneered the idea of solar zoning legislation and laws for protecting citizens' access to sunlight. With increasing urban density, the need to legislate solar access became evident in Roman cities. Soon complaints and lawsuits were initiated because many home owners aspired to incorporate a heliocaminus and, thus, needed unobstructed access to sunlight. Ulpian, a sitting judge from Rome in the second century AD, upheld the solar rights of plaintiffs, decreeing that access to sunlight should be upheld and guaranteed. As a result of this ruling, a legal precedent for solar rights was established and was later included in the Justinian Code of Law (Jordan and Perlin, 1979).

Figure 1.19   Oculus trapping the sun beams over the rotunda of the Pantheon in Rome (courtesy of Dreamstime).

1.5   THE INDUSTRIAL REVOLUTION AND THE MODERN AGE

During the mid-eighteenth century, the early years of the Industrial Revolution, Western Europe witnessed enormous economic and social changes as massive numbers of people migrated from rural areas to urban centers to seek work

Figure 1.20   The Baths of Caracalla built in Rome between AD 212 and AD 216 (courtesy of Dreamstime).

in the growing number of factories. Skyrocketing demands for housing due to the rapid and large influx of people led to overcrowded and unsanitary ghettos in many cities in Great Britain and in other countries of Western Europe. Immigrants found shelter in densely populated buildings, built back-to-back along narrow streets with open sewers and which offered little or no exposure to sunlight (Figures 1.21 and 1.22). The population of Manchester, for example, experienced heavy growth because the city was a center for the textile industry. Its population increased sixfold between 1771 and 1831 (Fisher, 1995). Architects produced cheap and

Figure 1.21 *Over London by Rail* Gustave Doré, *c.* 1870, shows the densely populated and polluted environments in the new industrial cities.

expedient solutions for an emerging housing shortage but poor sanitary facilities remained. Jacob's Island, one of the earliest and most notorious slums of the parish Bermondsey in London, exemplified these horrible living conditions. Its notoriety was noted by Charles Dickens in *Oliver Twist* as he described Bill Sykes' lair:

> there exists the filthiest, the strangest, the most extraordinary of the many localities that are hidden in London, wholly unknown, even by name, to the great mass of its inhabitants. To reach this place, the visitor has to penetrate through a maze of close, narrow, and muddy streets, thronged by the roughest and poorest of waterside people, and devoted to the traffic they may be supposed to occasion.

These deplorable living conditions led to outbreaks of cholera, typhus, rickets, tuberculosis, and other deadly plagues. The first epidemic of cholera registered in England was in the fall of 1831 in the town of Sunderland, but this outbreak was not unique to Great Britain. Others followed, in Germany and other parts of industrializing Western Europe. While the foul waters from open sewers provided the chief environment for the pathogens that caused these outbreaks

Figure 1.22 A street in Great Britain with an open sewer and damp conditions with no sunlight during the early–mid eighteenth century.

(Finer, 1952), the lack of sunlight in dwellings was noted as an exacerbating factor.

In the nineteenth century, reformers and planners concerned with poor urban sanitary conditions launched a movement to bring fresh air and sunlight to the slums that blighted European cities. Influenced by The Chadwick Report of 1842 on the sanitary conditions of the laboring population of Great Britain (Chadwick, 1842), the efforts of reformers grew in importance. For the first time in British history, the Public Health Act of 1848 charged the government with responsibility for the protection and safeguarding of public health and welfare. Commissioned by the government, Edwin Chadwick, secretary of the Poor Law Commission, issued proposals to resolve these problems. The report pointed out the correlation between disease, life expectancy, mortality rates, and the environment in which people lived. The following excerpts from the report make clear that correlation:

> That the various forms of epidemic, endemic, and other disease caused, or aggravated, or propagated chiefly amongst the labouring classes by atmospheric impurities produced by decomposing animal and vegetable substances, by damp and filth, and close and over-crowded dwellings prevail amongst the population in every part of the kingdom, whether dwelling in separate houses, in rural villages, in small towns, in the larger towns – as they have been found to prevail in the lowest districts of the metropolis.
>
> That such disease, wherever its attacks are frequent, is always found in connection with the physical circumstances above specified, and that where those circumstances are removed by drainage, proper cleansing, better ventilation, and other means of diminishing atmospheric impurity, the frequency and intensity of such disease is abated; and where the removal of the noxious agencies appears to be complete, such disease almost entirely disappears.
>
> That the annual loss of life from filth and bad ventilation are greater than the loss from death or wounds in any wars in which the country has been engaged in modern times.

New town planning and urban proposals emerged as a result of the work of Chadwick's Poor Law Commission and the efforts of others. In 1875, Benjamin W. Richardson (1876) issued plans for the utopian city he called *Hygeia*, or city of health. His plans incorporated increased numbers of green spaces and mandatory access to sunlight:

> Our city, which may be named Hygeia, has the advantage of being a new foundation, but it is so built that existing cities might be largely modeled upon it.
>
> The population of the city may be placed at 100,000, living in 20,000 houses, built on 4,000 acres of land – an average of twenty-five persons to an acre. This may be considered a large population for the space occupied, but, since the effect of density on vitality tells only determinately when it reaches a certain extreme degree, as in Liverpool and Glasgow, the estimate may be ventured.
>
> The safety of the population of the city is provided for against density by the character of the houses, which

ensure an equal distribution of the population. Tall houses overshadowing the streets, and creating necessity for one entrance to several tenements, are nowhere permitted. In streets devoted to business, where the trades people require a place of mart or shop, the houses are four stories high, and in some of the western streets where the houses are separate, three and four storied buildings are erected; but on the whole it is found bad to exceed this range, and as each story is limited to 15 feet, no house is higher than 60 feet.

Another town planning proposal came from Ebenezer Howard, who in 1898 published a book, *To-Morrow: A Peaceful Path to Real Reform,* which was reissued in 1902 under its present title, *Garden Cities of To-Morrow* (Howard, 1902). He called for the creation of new towns of limited size, planned in advance, and surrounded by a permanent belt of agricultural land. Howard's model became known as the 'Garden City' (Figure 1.23). It was

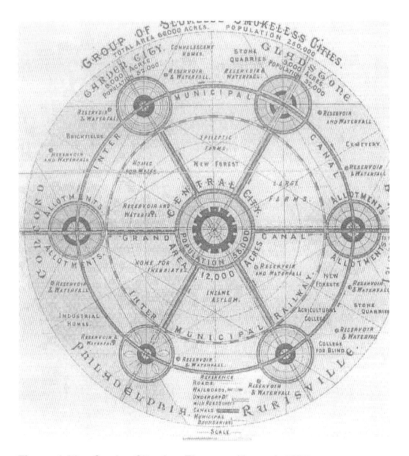

Figure 1.23 *Garden City plan*, Ebenezer Howard, 1898.

to be built near the center of 6000 acres, covering an area of 1000 acres, or 1/6th of the total acreage. As depicted diagrammatically in Figure 1.24, several boulevards traversed the city from center to circumference, dividing it into six equal parts or wards. In the center, a circular space containing about five and a half acres was laid out as green space and garden. Surrounding the garden were larger public buildings – the town hall, principal concert and lecture hall, theater, library, museum, picture gallery, and hospital. Several new towns, Welwyn and Letchworth among others, were built based on Howard's garden city model.

Not until the mid-nineteenth century did the design community and advocates for good lighting practices in buildings begin to be heard. The well-known aristocratic British nurse, Florence Nightingale, was an advocate for maximizing natural light and sunlight in people's homes and in hospital wards. She noted that patients on the sunny side of wards had higher spirits and were more cheerful than those in areas that didn't receive sunlight (Woodham-Smith, 1951). The Lady with the Lamp, as Florence Nightingale was known, went on to suggest architectural plans for hospital wards with shallow floor plans that would receive sunlight from two sides instead of one all the areas of the ward would have access to sunlight.

Awareness of the importance of light in people's lives grew when Dr Niels Finson received the Nobel Prize in 1903 for proving that sunlight can cure tuberculosis and for devising a method using ultraviolet therapy in the cure of lupus vulgaris (Holick, 1999). In the world of architecture, the early part of the twentieth century witnessed the birth of a new movement one that embraced modernity and rejected the old ways of designing buildings. Until then, buildings had been pastiches of past styles. They were dark and unhealthy with massive masonry structures and small windows. Technological advances spurred new ways of thinking about building design. Buildings could now be constructed with long spans and large openings. These innovations allowed architects, such as those of the Bauhaus School in Germany (Figure 1.25) and the De Stjil school in The Netherlands, as exemplified by the work of the Dutch architect Gerrit T. Rietveld (Figure 1.26), to adopt a totally new architecture. The Modern Movement gained popularity after World War II through the work of CIAM (Congrés International de l'Architecture Moderne) whose principles and theories were instrumental in planning and rebuilding devastated European cities. The work of Le Corbusier, Walter Gropius, and Mies van der Rohe embodied the underlying principles of CIAM and the Modern Movement in architecture.

This new architecture emphasized straight lines and simple, economic forms. It incorporated large expanses of windows

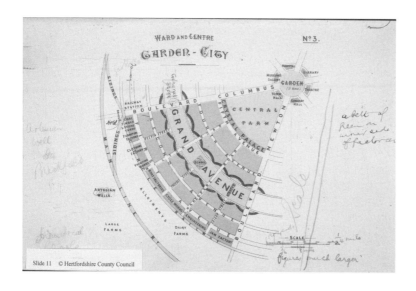

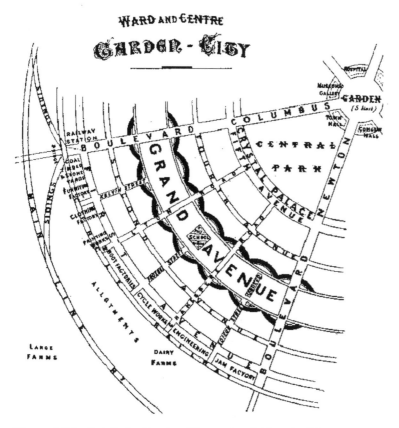

Figure 1.24 Detail of a Garden City ward as laid out by Ebenezer Howard.

Figure 1.25   The Bauhaus School, built 1925–1926 in Dessau, Germany (photo by Dreamstime).

Figure 1.26   The Schroder House, Utrecht, The Netherlands, Gerrit Thomas Rietveld (1924).

to maximize natural light and fresh air. Human scale in building design, along with proportion and ergonomics, were chief design principles of this new architecture. The new motto was 'Less is more' and new design principles included 'Le plan

Figure 1.27 Villa Savoye at Poissy, France, Le Corbusier, 1926 (courtesy of Botond Bognar).

libre' or the free plan, 'Form follows function,' and 'Truth to materials.' This new architecture was concerned with economy, hygiene, health, and the natural environment.

Le Corbusier, one of the most prominent architects of the Modern Movement, once stated that in addition to the three physical dimensions of any building, a fourth existed, namely nature. This dimension brought fresh air, sunlight, and health to the building occupants. One of his most well-known residential projects is La Villa Savoye at Poissy, France (Figure 1.27) where such CIAM concepts were crystallized as elevating the bulk of the building off the ground through the use of 'pilotis' and introducing the 'free façade' and the 'plan libre' where walls need not be load-bearing and could take free forms. Windows could then be made wider, allowing large spans of glass and ample natural light inside the building. Le Corbusier was known for the grand scale of his urban interventions, one of which was *La Ville Radieuse* of 1922 (Figure 1.28). This proposed utopian city for a population of three million would increase the urban capacity and at the same time improve the urban environment and the efficiency of the city. It would be divided into functional zones: twenty-four glass towers in the center would form the commercial district, separated from the industrial and residential districts by expansive green belts with *immeuble-villas* with access to green space and sunlight.

The simplicity and clarity of the Modern Movement ideology and the awareness of the importance of natural light in architecture can be found in work of such prominent architects as Richard Neutra, Frank Loyd Wright and Mies van der

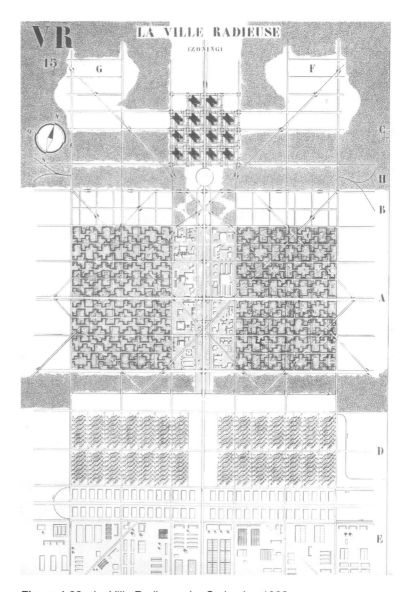

Figure 1.28 La Ville Radieuse, Le Corbusier, 1922.

Rohe. The latter designed the Farnsworth House in 1946, in Plano, Illinois (Figures 1.29 and 1.30), a transparent structure, expressing the importance of pure lines, clarity and calmness in a verdant landscape (Spaeth, 1985). Elevated off the ground, the Farnsworth House was contained within four glass walls through which daylight permeates the entire house, with no interior walls touching the exterior; a radical departure from houses of the time.

Running parallel to these new building concepts was the development of electric incandescent and fluorescent lamps

Figure 1.29 The Farnsworth House in Plano, Illinois by Mies van der Rohe, 1946.

Figure 1.30 The interior of the Farnsworth House in Plano, Illinois, by Mies van der Rohe, 1946 (by Mies van der Rohe).

in the late nineteenth century. With growing pressure from utility companies to increase the consumption of electricity, architects were urged to rely more and more on fluorescent light for building illumination. Economies of structure encouraged the lowering of ceilings, thereby reducing the volume of the building to be heated or cooled but also reducing the penetration of daylight. Many building professionals even argued that daylight was a luxury that could be disregarded altogether since fluorescent lighting could supply ample light economically. The emphasis on the energy efficiency of electric light soon prevailed over the use of daylighting. Natural light was all but abandoned, and the quantity of illumination became an obsession as research in lighting ergonomics indicated a direct relationship between productivity and lighting levels. Light levels as high as 1200 lux were adopted without regard to energy costs or the quality of the illumination. New building typologies emerged, giving rise to tall buildings with deep floor plans and low ceiling heights. Interior spaces no longer had to rely on natural light for workers and residents. By the 1960s factories and office buildings were built in which most of the workforce could be placed either away from windows or in spaces entirely without windows. With rising costs of land in major industrial cities, developers sought to optimize the land they owned and built taller and more massive structures. The result was overcrowded urban centers, particularly in the United States. The street canyons of New York City (Figure 1.31) receive little air and sunlight year round and are illustrative of the type of urbanization that began in the early

Figure 1.31 An example of overshadowed streets in New York City (courtesy of Jay Davidson).

twentieth century, accelerated through the late twentieth century, and continues today.

1.6 ENERGY CRISIS

The oil embargo and the energy crisis of 1973 led to increased interest in energy conservation and the use of renewable energy sources such as solar power. Solar architecture was a direct response to the oil crisis, and its popularity grew in the late 1970s, particularly in the American southwest where there is abundant sunlight. Passive solar design principles were soon adapted to climates beyond that of the American southwest, as new technologies emerged and know-how improved. As concern grew over the use of fossil fuels (oil, natural gas, and coal) to produce electricity, interest in the use of sunlight as an alternative source to meet some of the energy demands of buildings increased, albeit grudgingly.

The number of buildings that rely on the sun and other eco-friendly design principles to meet their energy demands remains minuscule compared with their conventional counterparts. As Figure 1.32 illustrates, the projected worldwide use of all energy sources increases through 2030. Fossil fuels will continue to supply much of the energy used worldwide, but projections indicate that the use of renewable energy will continue to expand.

Despite current calls for energy conservation, daylighting is rarely used as a significant strategy to reduce energy consumption. Because of the rate structure and billing systems

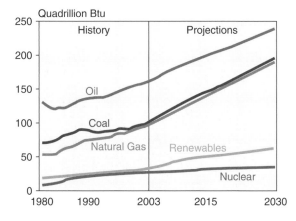

Figure 1.32   World market energy use by energy type, 1980–2030 (source: www.eia.doe.gov/iea).

of utility companies, which are concerned primarily with peak demand for electric power rather than total consumption, many buildings remain lit at night even when unoccupied. Many offices and stores continue to be lit during the day when there is no need for additional illumination. The fact is that calls for energy conservation have not significantly influenced architectural practice. Architects and engineers prefer to rely on mechanical and electrical equipment to illuminate and air condition buildings rather than to seek building materials and layouts that take advantage of what nature has to offer. So-called green or eco-friendly buildings remain a novelty in the architectural world, the subject of case studies and museum exhibits. Until we emphasize environmental concerns such as gas emissions and global warming, and until we demonstrate scientifically and tangibly its negative impact on the health and well-being of building occupants, the architectural and engineering approach to building design will remain technologically driven with little emphasis on a partnership with nature that favors the well-being of building occupants.

Daylighting legislation

Proponents of daylighting have focused primarily on its potential for energy savings in efforts to popularize its use. Because of technical innovations over the years, electric lighting equipment has become more energy efficient and lighting energy standards have reflected this. Despite this progress, however, lighting remains a major energy consumer in large buildings. According to the U.S. Electric Power Research Institute, in the United States' commercial sector an average of 37% of the electricity used is consumed by electric lighting (Energy Information Administration, 1998). Daylighting has the potential not only to reduce the amount of electric energy used for lighting but also to lower peak demand and reduce cooling loads caused by heat released into the space by the lighting fixtures. Despite these substantial benefits, daylighting is not a mainstream architectural feature in the majority of buildings. Some of its proponents suggest that the argument for daylighting should no longer be based on energy savings because that approach has not proved effective; rather, the argument should focus on the benefits of daylighting for health and well-being (Boubekri, 2004b).

Daylighting is not a commonplace design application because no compelling legislation mandates it. Daylighting legislation is beset by many problems, some germane to the general field of lighting and others more specific to the nature of daylight as a source of illumination. The spectral quality of daylight, which is difficult to duplicate artificially, makes it an almost entirely different type of light to that produced by any electric source. Anecdotal evidence suggests that, because of the superior qualities of daylight, less light may be needed than with electric light to perform the same visual tasks. This phenomenon is not completely understood however, and the nature of the source of daylight further complicates standardization. Daylight is dynamic, constantly changing in terms of intensity, direction, and color properties, and is unpredictable, and unreliable. The quantity of daylight available outdoors is time, location, and site specific. These qualities make the requirement for certain daylight levels inside a room a complicated issue. Though it is now possible to predict both exterior and interior daylight levels through empirical or simulation modeling techniques, outdoor daylight predictions are based on historical data collected over a long period of time. The calculated daylight levels, however, remain only statistical predictions and, thus, can neither be precise nor guaranteed. Moreover, we do not have all the tools needed to predict indoor daylight quantities for every possible design scenario. The theoretical algorithms to model the performance of a number of daylighting strategies do not as yet exist. Therefore, the only way to predict performance is through empirical simulation using scale modeling techniques, a solution that can be time-consuming and impractical for many designers.

A cursory overview of the legislation pertaining to daylighting shows that it varies from one country to another (Julian, 1998). Overall, it tends to be of three types. The first, and perhaps most practical, relates to the access buildings have to sunlight. This type of legislation, usually referred to as solar zoning legislation, attempts to guarantee buildings and their occupants access to sunlight for a predetermined length of time, usually by establishing local zoning ordinances that stipulate how high buildings can be and their set-backs from property lines. The second type of legislation relates to the requirement for windows and their sizes and is usually found in building codes. The third type relates to the quantity of indoor illumination inside a room.

2.1 SOLAR ZONING LEGISLATION

The idea of solar access is not new. It was practiced by the ancient Greeks and Romans during the classical periods as well as by other cultures at various times and in various places around the globe. In the United States, Native Americans valued solar access, as evidenced in the layered architecture of the pueblos of the American southwest. Formally speaking, however, and until the mid-nineteenth century, solar rights in the United States tended to be protected through the doctrine of Ancient Lights, which emanated from the Prescription Act of 1832, a British law that prevented a landowner from obstructing the sunlight of an adjoining landowner who had enjoyed uninterrupted sunlight through a window for twenty years. If a landowner had gained the right to Ancient Lights, the owner of the adjoining land could not obscure them by erecting a new building. If the neighbor did so, he or she could be sued under a clause of nuisance.

A more formal interpretation of solar zoning evolved from the concept of the *solar envelope* (Knowles, 1980; Smith, 1983) by which the form of a building is determined in relation to its ability to let sunshine into the street (Figure 2.1). This type of legislation is dictated by local socio-economic, cultural, and political forces and is addressed by local authorities, not only from one country to another but from one municipality to another or even from areas within a given municipality. Such legislation generally impacted building bulks, heights, and set-backs from property lines.

Solar zoning legislation in the United States is rooted in the 1916 Zoning Ordinance of New York City (New York City Department of City Planning, 2004), one of the first cities to document provisions for solar access. The case of New York City was unique because of the huge demand for land in Manhattan. In the early 1900s, with the advent of steel technology accompanied by the high cost of land in Manhattan, many developers maximized the use of the land they owned by building tall and massive buildings. Many such buildings were built in this period by large corporations as advertising symbols of power and corporate image. At this point, the need for height and bulk regulations for larger buildings became a pressing issue for residents and politicians alike. The decision to regulate became final in 1915 with

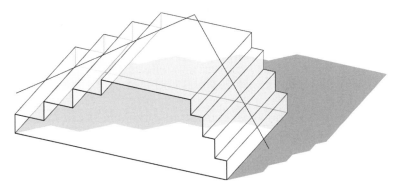

Figure 2.1   The sun angles defining the building envelope within which the building structure is contained.

Figure 2.2   The Equitable Life Assurance building in New York City built in 1915, Ernest R. Graham & Associates (courtesy of Scott Murphy).

the completion of the Equitable Life Assurance building in lower Manhattan (Figure 2.2). Prior to its construction, many opposed this 40-story 1.4 million square foot building that covered an entire city block. Their efforts failed to stop the construction of this massive building that cast a permanent shadow over much of the financial district.

The Equitable building caused considerable public outcry. People became more conscious of the importance of sunlight in their daily lives as connections were made between epidemics such as rickets and tuberculosis and the lack of sunlight in the working and living environment. The issue of air and light became a health issue and was expressed as the 'inalienable right to air and light.' These concerns led to the

Figure 2.3   Sky exposure from street level based on the concept of how much of the sky is available from the street (courtesy of Dreamstime).

1916 zoning ordinance that covered three major areas, each of which depended on the 'sky exposure plane' (Figure 2.3), a concept based on the angle from the center of the street to the top of the building (Figure 2.4). Because of formal requirements regarding the need for sun penetration and a view of the sky from the street, the trademark 'wedding cake' architecture of New York City came into being (Figures 2.5 and 2.6).

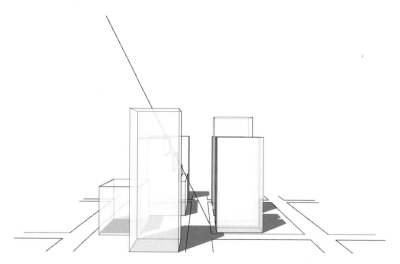

Figure 2.4   Set-back following a sun angle from the median along the street level.

The 1916 zoning ordinance was amended in 1961 and gave occupants access to light and air through the creation of publicly accessible exterior plazas (Kwartler and Masters, 1984). It also granted incentives to developers to provide these plazas in return for an added increment of floor area on their sites.

Solar zoning legislation varies from one country to another and is the outcome of cultural, economic, and social forces. In Japan, for instance, such legislation relates to public health, safety, and welfare and recognizes the need to protect the environment and to preserve limited natural resources (Miller, 1976). Access to the sun in Japan is hardly a modern issue. As early as the Tokugawa period (1600 to 1868), owners of trees paid *kage-shiro*, or 'shade-money,' to their neighbors if their trees shadowed the ridge of the neighbor's roof (Wigmore, 1971). A neighbor who planted a tree or built a tall structure would be required as a matter of social practice to pay a 'shade penalty' (*kage-shik*) as compensation for the obstruction of sunlight (Takagi, 1977–1978). Judicial recognition of a person's right to the sun did not, however, become a legal matter until the mid and late 1960s when the density of Japanese cities increased. *Nissho-ken*, the right to sunlight, is the term used to reflect the growing desire for the legal protection of solar rights.

Over the last four decades and particularly since the energy crisis of the 1970s, solar access in many countries has become the focus of political and legal discussion. It is

Figure 2.5 Wedding-cake style of building resulting from the 1916 zoning ordinance in New York City (courtesy of Scott Murphy).

an even more pertinent issue today as the world focuses on global warming, climate change, and the search for ways to lessen reliance on fossil fuels. These concerns, coupled with issues of health and well-being, make solar access an even more relevant and important area of public policy (Knowles, 1979).

Figure 2.6   Wedding-cake style of building resulting from the 1916 zoning ordinance in New York City (courtesy of Dreamstime).

2.2   LEGISLATION BASED ON WINDOW SIZE

The most frequently used legislation that relates, albeit indirectly, to daylighting is the requirement for specific window sizes for various types of spaces. Such requirements, however, are not intended to supply daylight but rather to facilitate the venting of smoke or to provide exits in case of fire or other emergencies.

Building codes worldwide generally prescribe a minimum percentage of the floor area of the room, or exceptionally of the area of the wall containing the window, that the window must be. In England, for example, the British Code BR 8206 recommends that windows be, at a minimum, 20% of the external window wall for rooms measuring less than 8 meters in depth and 35% of the external wall for rooms deeper than 14 meters (Department of the Environment, 1971; Health & Safety Commission, 1992). For offices, windows should account for 35% of the exposed wall area; in institutional buildings the requirement is 25% (Littlefair, 1999).

Australia's building code requires a window size equal to 10% of the floor area for habitable rooms in residential buildings (Australia Community Development Project, 2002). In Japan, regulations for the size of windows apply only to buildings with continuous occupancy such as houses, schools, or hospitals. Industrial and office buildings are not considered to fit this category and therefore have no minimum window size requirements (Koga and Nakamura, 1998). According to Koga and Nakamura (1998), article 28 of the Japanese building code stipulates that habitable rooms in continuous occupancy buildings should have window sizes no less than 14% or 1/7th of the total floor area of the building and between 20% and 40% of the floor area in other types of buildings. Article 20 of the same code prescribes the method to be used in calculating window size.

In the United States, the Building Official Code Administrators (BOCA) specifies that every room or space intended for human occupancy should have an exterior glazing area of not less than 8% of the total floor area. Where natural light for rooms and spaces is provided through an adjacent room, the opening within the wall separating these two spaces must be no less than 8% of the total floor area of the room (BOCA, 1990).

2.3 QUANTITY OF ILLUMINATION LEGISLATION

Because daylight is dynamic, changing throughout the day and from season to season, the quantity of indoor and outdoor illumination is time-dependent. Consequently, we cannot prescribe daylight levels inside a room without considering the duration of illumination. Attempts at requiring a certain level of natural light in buildings just about anywhere around the world have been at best sketchy due, in no small measure, to this fact (Boubekri, 2004a).

Illuminance-based standards

Illuminance-based requirements are usually in the form of recommended practices targeting the minimum illuminance level necessary to perform specific visual tasks. In the United States, the Illuminating Engineering Society of North America (IESNA) sets these standards. It has established a set of minimum recommended illuminance levels for a variety of visual tasks and space functions. IESNA has no daylighting requirements. The IESNA daylighting committee has established a set of recommended practices for daylighting which are revised from time to time, but these are neither mandatory nor do they specify target illuminance levels of daylight. BOCA (1990), the organization responsible for the national building code, stipulates that

> the standard for natural light for all habitable and occupiable rooms shall be based on 250 foot-candles (2691 lux) of illumination on the vertical plane adjacent to the exterior of the light-transmitting device in the enclosure wall and shall be adequate to provide an average illumination of 6 foot-candles (64.58 lux) over the area of the room at a height of 30 inches (762 mm) above the floor level.

Such illuminance levels must be supplied to all habitable spaces except for crawl spaces beneath buildings or in attics. These levels can be supplied by electric light.

The Department of Public Works of Canada, the federal organization responsible for the government's internal servicing and administration, recommends an average daylight level of 200 lux along the perimeter of office space at a depth of 3 meters for 80% of business hours during a regular 8:00 a.m. to 5:00 p.m. schedule (Archer, 1998; Wotton, 1998). However, these are only recommended levels, not enforceable by law.

In France, requirements for lighting workplaces can be found in the *Decret no.83-722* of August 2, 1983, concerning general lighting and in *Lettre-circulaire DRT no.90/11* of June 28, 1990, relative to daylighting and the provision of views of the outdoors. Daylight levels are not mandatory but are preferred or recommended. The *Lettre-circulaire DRT no.90/11* of 1990 stipulates

> In general and for new construction, daylight coming from side and overhead apertures must be usable in workspaces, but there aren't any minimal levels that are required.

The *Lettre circulaire DRT 90/11* is, however, much more explicit when it comes to the provision of views

> Spaces destined for work must have transparent apertures at eye level with view towards the exterior, unless windows are incompatible with the type of activity that is taking place in that space. Interior workstations must be protected from unwanted direct solar radiation ...

Daylight factor-based standards

The Daylight Factor (DF) is defined as the percentage of horizontal indoor illuminance in relation to the outdoor illuminance on the ground under an overcast sky condition, as defined by the Commission Internationale de l'Eclairage (CIE). DF-based legislation does not target a specific daylight illuminance level in a room because of constantly changing outdoor conditions; rather, it is based on a percentage of whatever daylight is available outside and therefore is more practical than illuminance-based legislation. An example of such legislation can be found in a few countries. In France, the *Cahier des Recommendations Techniques de Construction* (Ministère d'Education, 1977) recommends a minimum DF in classrooms of 1.5% under overcast sky conditions. In the United Kingdom during the post-war era, government regulation prescribed a minimum DF of 2% in classrooms. This regulation was subsequently dropped when it became apparent that it is not always possible to meet the 2% target when a room has windows on only one side. To achieve the 2% target, windows would have had to be so large that they might have caused other problems, such as overheating in the summer, excessive glare, or other kinds of visual discomfort. Currently no daylighting legislation exists in the United Kingdom but only a set of recommendations established by the Building Research Establishment (British Standard Institute, 1982), which allows some flexibility in the way planners and architects may use these recommendations in zoning and site planning. A 27% Vertical Sky Component opening is recommended as an acceptable level of light for a window to receive. This level is based on a window looking across a 12-meter-wide street at a typical terraced house with ground and first floor levels. Within an inner city center, the 27% Vertical Sky Component cannot always be achieved. This standard, therefore, mainly applies to residential buildings and such habitable rooms as living rooms, dining rooms, studies, kitchens, and bedrooms.

This cursory overview of daylighting standards makes clear the deficiency of building codes in regard to daylighting. If we think of daylighting as the active use of daylight in building interiors to achieve a particular purpose, then no daylighting standards that are enforceable by law exist in any country. Legislation that mandates minimum window sizes for certain types of spaces cannot be considered daylighting legislation because it does not necessarily translate into the actual presence of daylight inside a room as a window may have a very low daylight transmission coefficient. In most cases, window-size legislation is meant to provide means of egress and ventilation in case of fire and other emergencies.

Although several countries, for example Germany, The Netherlands, and Canada, have made recommendations for daylighting, none has made them mandatory. To be credible, daylighting legislation should prescribe light levels inside a room for a given duration throughout the day according to the season, the climate, and the function of the space. Such legislation would inevitably push the boundaries of creativity and encourage designers and architects to position and size building openings and to select appropriate optical properties of windows. Only then could the function of windows be counted as genuinely having a daylighting role distinct from the more traditional roles of providing a view or ventilation.

Seasonal Affective Disorder, depression, and their relationship to daylight

3.1 LIGHT AND THE HUMAN ENDOCRINE SYSTEM

Light affects our bodies in two ways. In the first, light impinges on the retina of our eyes and, through our vision system, affects our metabolism and our endocrine and hormone systems. In the second, it interacts with our skin by way of photosynthesis and produces vitamin D.

Most of our body's life-sustaining functions are controlled by the hypothalamus, an area of the brain below the thalamus (Figure 3.1). The hypothalamus is responsible for a number of metabolic processes and for such autonomic activities as energy and fluid balance, growth and maturation, circulation, breathing, emotional balance, reproduction, heat regulation, and the circadian cycle. It links the nervous system to the endocrine system by synthesizing and secreting neurohormones as needed; these in turn control the secretion of hormones from the anterior pituitary gland (Figure 3.2).

Our daily activity and sleep rhythms are regulated by a control center in the hypothalamus called the suprachaismatic nucleus (SCN), also known as the body clock. The body clock needs to receive signals to tell it when to shut down and prepare for sleep and when to produce the active waking

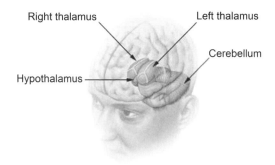

Figure 3.1   The hypothalamus part of the brain.

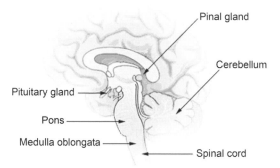

Figure 3.2   The pineal and pituitary glands in the brain.

hormones. It generally requires daily resetting by external time cues. This process is called entrainment. The day–night cycle of a 24-hour solar day is the main environmental signal entraining the clock and the rhythms driven by it. Our body must receive these cues with the right amount of light at the right time and frequency. When it doesn't, the internal clock is disturbed, and so are many of our bodily functions.

The most powerful signal is bright light, such as sunshine (Moore and Eichler, 1972; Stephan and Zucker,1972; Inouye and Kawamura, 1979). The SCN serves as an hourglass timer or a pacemaker for our internal clock or circadian rhythm and is directly influenced by light intensity. Daylight serves as a catalyst for the secretion of hormones from the pineal gland (Figure 3.2), namely serotonin and melatonin. The level of melatonin determines the energy and activity levels in our bodies. At darkness or low light levels, melatonin secretion increases and drowsiness occurs. Daylight suppresses the production of melatonin and fosters an alert state of mind by secreting serotonin. People who live and work in window-less environments or in places lacking adequate light may be at risk of having their internal clock continually disturbed.

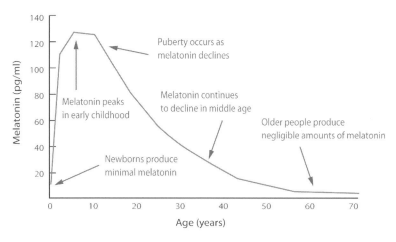

Figure 3.3   Variation of melatonin secretion with age.

Melatonin, the so-called 'natural nightcap,' directly acts on the SCN to influence circadian rhythms (Weaver *et al.*, 1993). At night melatonin is produced to help our bodies regulate our light–dark diurnal cycles. Melatonin is an important anti-oxidant and can neutralize some agents (the hydroxyl radical agents) that damage cells and DNA that are believed to be a contributing cause of some internal cancers (Reiter, 1995).

Serotonin, a hormone first discovered in 1933, is the neuro-transmitter identified in many psychiatric disorders including depression, anorexia, bulimia, obsessive-compulsive disor-der, and social anxiety. Serotonin is an important regulator of these disorders. If we compare the brain to a car engine, serotonin can be considered the 'oil' of the brain. During long periods of high stress, serotonin is used up, exceeding its replenishment rate. Prolonged stress lowers serotonin levels in the brain and a stress-induced depression may take place. The less serotonin available in the brain, the more severe is the depression and related symptoms. Low serotonin func-tion is thought to result in a type of depression characterized by such symptoms as suicidal thoughts and feelings of sad-ness, worthlessness, and guilt.

The actions of serotonin and melatonin on our circadian rhythm function in opposition, with serotonin stimulating us during the daytime and melatonin inducing sleep at night; however, they should be seen as complementary to each other and equally essential to our circadian rhythm. Healthy young and middle-aged adults usually secrete about 5 to 25 micrograms of melatonin each night. The levels peak at ages 2 to 5 years and then progressively decline by 10–15% per decade (Figure 3.3) (Brown *et al.*, 1979; Waldhauser *et al.*, 1984; Zhdanova *et al.*, 1998; Grivas and Savvidou, 2007).

Scientists speculate that this decline may explain why young people have fewer problems sleeping than older people.

3.2 DAYLIGHT AND SEASONAL AFFECTIVE DISORDER

The seasonal depression often found among people living in northern latitudes and typically referred to as Seasonal Affective Disorder (SAD) is a commonly known effect of light that is related to our endocrinal system. The term was first used by Dr Norman E. Rosenthal in 1981 to describe the depression brought about by lack of daylight. SAD is an emotional disorder characterized by drastic mood swings, lowered energy, and depression.

According to Avery and colleagues (2001), more than 10% of the population of Finland and about 6% of that of the United States suffer from this seasonal disorder. The highest occurrence of SAD is found in the northernmost parts of the United States, between 45° and 50° north latitude. We know that melatonin levels in those experiencing SAD are higher than normal during the day, so sufferers experience sleepiness, fatigue, and other melatonin-induced effects. They are also prone to symptoms of serotonin deficiency such as negative emotional states and poor performance.

Table 3.1 shows the number of daylight hours for 40°, 45°, and 50° north latitude for each month of the year, as well as the number of daylight hours in addition to the 8 hours of a typical work day (8 a.m. to 5 p.m. solar time). A worker would be exposed to one hour of daylight during midday in the months of November, December, and January. For another two months (October and February) there would be approximately three hours of daylight outside the working day, assuming a one-hour break at midday. It is worth noting that the hours of daylight shown in Table 3.1 were computed as soon as the solar altitude angle was greater than zero, even though the amount of daylight available at the beginning and the end of each day might have been totally insignificant. Therefore, in practical terms, the total number of daily daylight hours may be less than those indicated in the table.

Webb and Puig-Domingo (1995) describe SAD as

> a depression occurring in the winter months and associated with insomnia, weight gain and craving for carbohydrate ... found to improve with bright light treatment.

Rosenthal and colleagues (1984) found that the improvement in their patients' depression appeared to be related to

Table 3.1 Compiled data showing total daylight hours (DH) per day on the 21st of each month and the daylight hours outside of an 8 hour (8 a.m.–5 p.m) work schedule with a one-hour lunch break at midday.

	40°N latitude		45°N latitude		50°N latitude	
	Total DH	DH outside 8 a.m.–5 p.m. work schedule	Total DH	DH outside 8 a.m.–5 p.m. work schedule	Total DH	DH outside 8 a.m.–5 p.m. work schedule
January	9	1	9	1	9	1
February	11	3	11	3	11	3
March	12	4	12	4	12	4
April	13	5	13	5	13	5
May	15	7	15	7	15	7
June	15	7	15	7	17	9
July	15	7	15	7	15	7
August	13	5	13	5	13	5
September	13	5	13	5	13	5
October	11	3	11	3	11	3
November	9	1	9	1	9	1
December	9	1	9	1	7	1

light rather than to melatonin inhibition, because the suppression of melatonin through medication did not reduce depression.

Investigations into the role of serotonin in depression and mood disorders have been taking place for more than 30 years. Researchers Arthur J. Prange, Jr, of the University of North Carolina at Chapel Hill (Prange *et al.*, 1974) and Alec Coppen of the Medical Research Council in England along with their co-workers are credited with pioneering work in this area and were the first to formulate what is known as the 'permissive hypothesis' in the field of depression. This means that the synaptic depletion of serotonin causes depression by promoting, or 'permitting,' levels of the hormone neurotransmitter norepinephrine to fall. Slow serotonin secretion may also account for the emotional, appetite, libido, and sleep disturbances associated with depression.

Since light intensity is a catalyst for serotonin, there are reasons to believe that daylight deficiency could cause such disorders. Research has established a direct correlation between the degree of vulnerability to SAD and exposure to natural light. It is widely held that higher levels of melatonin caused by fewer hours of daylight contribute to this disorder. SAD patients report that their depression worsens whenever the sky is overcast at any time of the year and/or their indoor lighting is decreased (Nayyar and Cochrane, 1996). SAD sufferers living in northern latitudes note that their winter depressions become more severe the farther north they live (Lam *et al.*, 2001). Working in a windowless environment or in spaces that are deprived of adequate daylight may induce SAD. The close balance between serotonin and melatonin must therefore be maintained in order for our internal clock to function properly.

So how much light do we need?

Bright light therapy (Figure 3.4) to treat SAD was used for the first time by Rosenthal and his colleagues (1984). Their patient had a 13-year history of winter depression that would unexpectedly end when spring began. The initial approach of this first experimental therapy was to 'lengthen' the winter days by exposing the patient to bright light between 6 a.m. and 9 a.m. and between 4 p.m. and 7 p.m. However, this light therapy was an effective antidepressant only when the light was bright; dim light had no effect whatsoever. The early versions of a daylight-simulating full-spectrum light box emitted 2500 lux, which is five to ten times what most people receive from electric lights in their indoor working environments.

Skeptics have questioned whether this effect is in fact real or whether it is due to a placebo effect. In other words, is the effect simply due to the expectation of improvement or is

Figure 3.4 Bright light therapy lamp used to treat Seasonal Affective Disorder, providing 10 000 lux at a distance of 25 cm (photo Wikepedia public domain).

bright light therapy a true antidepressant? This question was answered by Eastman and colleagues (1998) who were able to determine that morning light of 6000 lux at 6 a.m. administered during a 3-week period produced the highest remission rate compared with that of an evening light of 6000 lux at 9 p.m. administered for an equal period of time or a placebo administered at 6 a.m. for an equal period of time.

Subsequent studies have found that the effectiveness of light therapy depends not only on the intensity of the light but also on the duration of exposure and the spectral quality (color appearance in terms warmth or coolness of the light; Wirz-Justice, 1998; Graw *et al.*, 1998). For example, two hours of treatment with 2500 lux per day may have an antidepressant effect equivalent to that of 30 minutes per day at 10 000 lux.

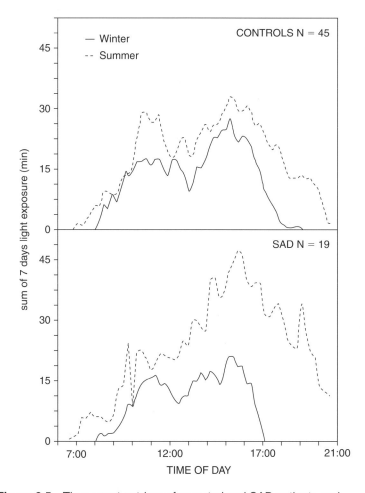

Figure 3.5   Time spent outdoors for control and SAD patients and healthy subjects (Graw *et al.*, *Journal of Affective Disorders* 56 (1999) 163–69).

Researchers now speculate that light therapy can be effective for 80% of SAD sufferers, but they also suggest that inadequate light intensity may not be the only explanation for SAD. The length of exposure to daylight levels outdoors in different seasons was hypothesized as a factor in SAD. Results from a study by Graw and his colleagues (1999) depicted in (Figure 3.5) show time spent outdoors for one week during summer and one week during winter. Little difference was observed between SAD sufferers and control subjects during summer but a significant difference was observed during winter. SAD sufferers spent much less time outdoors during the winter (47% of the time spent in summer). Although healthy people also tended to spend less time outdoors in the winter than in the summer, they spent more time outdoors than did SAD sufferers (67% of the time spent in summer). It appears that seasonal variations in the time people spend outdoors may be a factor for experiencing SAD, in addition to the intensity of light. Therefore the less the exposure to daylight levels and to the high light-intensity levels of daylight, the more acute is SAD.

3.3   STRESS AND ANXIETY IN RELATION TO DAYLIGHT

Cortisol, known also as the 'stress hormone,' is a corticosteroid hormone produced by the adrenal cortex. It follows a diurnal pattern with high values during the day and low values at night (Hollwich, 1979; Scheer and Buijs, 1999). It also exhibits a seasonal variation, with more stress hormones produced in summer than in winter (Erikson and Kuller, 1983; Kuller and Lindsten, 1992).

Abnormally high levels of cortisol increase blood pressure and blood sugar levels, may cause infertility in women, and suppress the immune system. At normal levels cortisol is involved in proper glucose metabolism, regulation of blood pressure, insulin release for blood sugar maintenance, and a healthy functioning immune system. Too much or too little cortisol has been implicated in numerous illnesses ranging from depression, cancer, and AIDS, to Alzheimer's disease (Sapse, 1997). Our body needs cortisol but only in the right amount.

Awakening is a strong stimulus to cortisol secretion and this awakening is influenced by light (Scheer and Buijs, 1999; Leproult et al., 2001). Office personnel working close to a window were found to have higher levels of morning cortisol during summer than during winter because daylight suppresses the production of melatonin and stimulates the secretion of cortisol, making people feel more alert and active, according to a study by Erikson and Kuller (1983). Daylight intensities found in the morning produce optimal levels of serotonin to engender a state of high alertness but not stress. Year-long observation of school children by Kuller and Lindsten (1992) indicated that high values of cortisol during winter correlated with low rates of absence because of illness. Moreover, high values of morning cortisol were associated with an inclination towards sociability and alertness. These findings explain why students with adequate exposure to daylight performed better than students with less exposure, as will be seen in Chapter 5.

Clearly, light acts on the production of cortisol, serotonin, and melatonin, three important hormones that affect our internal clock and our mood states, among many other effects. It is important to keep these hormones in proper balance. Low levels of serotonin (the daylight hormone) together with a low level of norepinephrine cause depression. Sluggish serotonin secretion may also account for the emotional, appetite, libido, and sleep disturbances associated with depression. Light therapy, be it artificial or natural, has been found to be an effective antidepressant but only when the light is bright enough. A proportional relationship exists between the intensity of light and the effectiveness of the therapy: 10000 lux worked three times faster than 2500 lux in alleviating winter depression. Researchers now speculate that by using light as a therapeutic agent, 80% of SAD sufferers can be cured. Studies, as we have noted, have also found that the effectiveness of light therapy depends not only on the intensity of light but also on the duration of exposure and its spectral quality. One can conclude that because of its numerous positive attributes, natural light is one of the best antidepressant agents available, one that is more efficient than electric light. It is almost impossible to illuminate a building with light at levels of 2500 lux or even 10000 lux, that combat depression. Such illumination, however, can be achieved with natural light. On a sunny day, the illuminance outside can be as high as 100000 lux and on a cloudy day it may reach 20000 lux. What is interesting to point out to architects is that we spend the majority of our lifetime indoors because of weather and the necessities of work. It is, therefore, all the more important for architects to design buildings that provide therapeutic light levels, preferably with daylight. Buildings should be designed not only as places for shelter and to house necessary activities but also as places for healing.

Traditional daylighting solutions relying on windows in the walls only, the solution adopted nowadays by builders of most multistory buildings, are very limited when it comes to alleviating SAD. The high levels of daylight that people require are confined to the peripheral area that is barely a few feet deep, normally not exceeding one and half times the height of the window. Daylight levels drop precipitously as one moves away from the window. Other more innovative solutions are needed to bring high levels of daylight to the central areas of the building and to the areas where the majority of workers are located most of the day. Light levels can drop by 50% or more by simply moving a few feet away from the window. Of course, it is possible to supplement the high light levels needed to combat SAD by using electric light, but with concerns about the depletion of fossil fuels and global warming, that solution may prove too costly. It falls, therefore, on architects to design buildings where daylight is plentiful throughout the building interior, not just the periphery. These high light levels should fall on the occupant's eyes, the first receptor in the light therapy process. Architects should concern themselves with furniture layouts that encourage building occupants to face windows instead of walls to maximize the effectiveness of light therapy.

Natural light and health

4

4.1 SUNLIGHT AND VITAMIN D

Definition and history of vitamin D

The first scientific description of a vitamin D deficiency, rickets, was provided in the seventeenth century (Whistler, 1645; Glisson, 1650). The healing effects of vitamin D, however, were not understood until the beginning of the twentieth century, the period between 1910 and 1930 when researchers were trying to identify the causes of rickets, an abnormal bone formation in children that results from inadequate bone calcium. Rickets is due to the failure to mineralize bone, thus causing osteomalacia, the softening of the bone structure. A dietary agent in cod liver oil was found to alleviate this problem and was named vitamin D. In 1923 an anti-rickets effect similar to that of cod liver oil was observed in ultraviolet (UV) radiation. Goldblatt and Soames (1923) observed that when a precursor of vitamin D in the skin, known as 7-dehydrocholesterol, was irradiated with sunlight or ultraviolet light, a substance

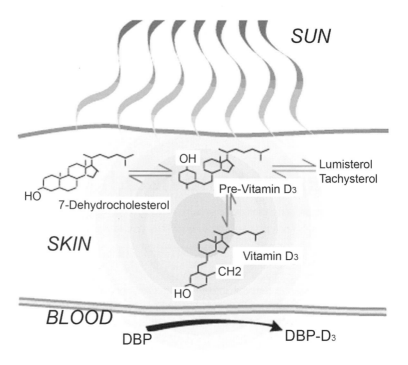

Figure 4.1   Vitamin D production through skin photosynthesis.

equivalent to vitamin D was produced. Vitamin D comprises a group of fat-soluble seco-sterols, scarce in most foods but manufactured in the skin of vertebrates through photosynthesis of solar ultraviolet type B radiation (UV-B).

Ultraviolet light is divided into three wavelength spectra: UV-A, UV-B, and UV-C. The shortest and most potent of the three, UV-C (<280 nm), can burn the skin even at small doses. It is completely absorbed by the ozone layer. UV-A (320 nm to 400 nm), known as 'black light,' has a longer wavelength than B or C and is responsible for skin darkening and pigmentation; consequently, we refer to it as the tanning light. UV-B (290 nm to 315 nm) is responsible for photosynthesis and stimulates our skin to produce vitamin D (Figure 4.1). It is also responsible for skin burning and aging. The amount of UV-B present in UV light depends on the angle of incidence of the solar rays and is most prevalent during midday hours at higher latitudes (Figure 4.2). The content of UV-B rays in sunshine is greatest at latitudes of up to 30 degrees north and south of the equator. At an altitude of 1000 meters the content of UV-B rays is 15% higher, whereas the content of UV-A rays is almost the same as at sea level. At latitudes greater than 55 degrees, very little UV-B radiation reaches the earth's surface during the winter months.

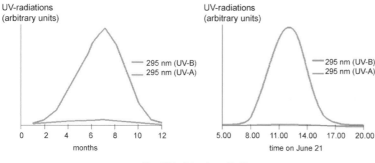

site: Washington, D.C.

Figure 4.2 Variation of UV radiation according to months and time of day (adapted from Serafino and Frederick, 1987; courtesy of William B. Grant).

A much higher proportion of UV energy passes through glass from daylight radiation than from incandescent, halogen, or fluorescent light sources. Glass, however, filters out about 95% of the UV-B radiation present in the atmosphere. As a result, the occupants of buildings receive nine to ten times less UV-B radiation than if they were outside.

Role of vitamin D

Vitamin D regulates the absorption of nutrients in the small intestine and their re-absorption in the kidneys. It helps maintain serum calcium and phosphorus concentrations within the normal range, thereby enhancing the capability of the small intestine to absorb these minerals from the diet. Both calcium and phosphorus are essential elements for the growth and development of bone structure (DeLuca, 1988; Reichel *et al.*, 1989). The absorption of these minerals enables bones and teeth to harden by increasing the deposition of calcium and assists in the migration of calcium across body cell membranes. The vitamin D compound has a brief residence time in the blood as it is normally stored either in fat or metabolized in the liver (Mawer *et al.*, 1972).

Vitamin D is essential for proper bone development and growth. We receive 80–100% of our vitamin D needs through our skin by way of photosynthesis (Glerup *et al.*, 2000). Vitamin D is called the 'sunshine vitamin' because it is formed in the skin by the action of ultraviolet rays from the sun.

In addition to the vitamin D we receive from the sun, it can also be found in foods such as eggs, meat, some cereals, oily fish, butter, and margarine. However, the dietary contribution to our vitamin D need is very small, if not negligible, compared with the amount produced through photosynthesis. It is, therefore, imperative that we receive adequate exposure to sunlight whether outdoors or indoors. Since we spend more than to 80% of our lifetime indoors (Newton *et al.*, 2001), architects are responsible for providing this vital ingredient to the occupants of buildings.

4.2   SUNLIGHT AND HYPOVITAMINOSIS D

According to an old adage, where sunlight goes the doctor does not. Our ancestors spent considerable time in the sun, but our relationship with the sun has changed over time as a result of modern working conditions, urbanization, and population migrations from rural to urban areas. This process began with the Industrial Revolution in the mid-eighteenth century. Today many of us spend the majority of our lifetime indoors, particularly in the industrialized world where the economy is industry- and service-based rather than based on agriculture. Most workers spend at least 5 days a week indoors at their workplace when daylight is at its peak. Because of its importance in the production of vitamin D, sunlight is vital to human life. When sunlight is inadequate, vitamin D levels decline, thereby provoking or exacerbating a number of health problems including bone thinning, many forms of cancer, high blood pressure, depression, and such immune-system disorders as multiple sclerosis, rheumatoid arthritis, and diabetes (Stein, 2004).

A variety of factors can limit our exposure to sunlight. We may not have access to adequate amounts of sunlight because our mobility is limited through age or illness, or because of the built environment in which we live and work. These conditions limit exposure to sunlight and cause a deficiency in vitamin D (hypovitaminosis D). Various reports suggests that more than 40% of American adults have low blood levels of vitamin D, a condition found among people living in northern latitudes above 30°N or in the southern latitudes above 30°S.

Patients who are hospitalized for prolonged periods are also known to be deficient in vitamin D. To examine this claim, a group of researchers from Massachusetts General Hospital and the Harvard Medical School (Giovannucci, 1998) assessed vitamin D intake, ultraviolet-light exposure, measured levels of serum 25-hydroxyvitamin D, parathyroid hormone, and ionized calcium in 290 patients on a general medical ward. A total of 57% (164 patients) were found to be vitamin D deficient, with serum concentration of 25-hydroxyvitamin D less than 25 ng/ml. Of these 164 patients, 64% were considered severely deficient. The study concluded that hypovitaminosis D is fairly common among hospital patients, not for dietary reasons but because of their limited exposure to sunlight due to restricted mobility and the inability to move about freely.

Seasonal variation in vitamin D is another strong indicator of the link between the degree of exposure to sunlight and vitamin D. Seasonal variations in serum 25-hydroxyvitamin D levels were found in a study conducted by a group of Italian medical researchers (Romagnoli *et al.*, 1999). Serum mean values were higher in summer in all groups, except in patients with longer hospitalization times. In each group, significantly higher prevalence of hypovitaminosis D was observed in winter than in summer, but once again long-term hospital patients experienced hypovitaminosis D in both winter and summer because their access to sunlight was restricted.

Cultural and geographical factors can also be causes for vitamin D deficiency. According to a health research forum in the United Kingdom (Gillie, 2006), 50% of people in Britain and Ireland were deficient in vitamin D because of climate conditions. It is worth noting that people from those countries who went on holiday to sunny climes more frequently exhibited less deficiency. A number of reports of vitamin D deficiency among Indo-Asians after migration to the United Kingdom was found to be related to inadequate sunlight (Iqbal *et al.*, 1994; Serhan *et al.*, 1999), a finding that indicates a strong link between sunlight and vitamin D and a weaker one between diet and vitamin D.

Women in countries of the Arabian Gulf region who totally cover their bodies, including their face and hands, were found to suffer from a more severe vitamin D deficiency than their western counterparts (El-Sonbaty and Abdul-Ghaffar 1996; Ghannam *et al.*, 1999; Gannage-Yared *et al.*, 2000; Saadi and Dawodu, 2005; Saadi *et al.*, 2006). Low exposure of the skin to sunlight because of dress code seems to be a major contributing factor to vitamin D deficiency. Although this condition could be partially due to dietary factors, hypovitaminosis D caused by lack of sunlight is believed to be a major contributing factor because we receive most of our vitamin D from sun-induced photosynthesis and not from diet. Similar results were obtained in a study that examined whether the latitudinal variation between Turkey and Germany and the wearing of the veil affected vitamin D levels in Turkish migrant populations in Germany (Erkal *et al.*, 2006). Turkish women in Germany experienced lower vitamin D levels than their female counterparts in Turkey where sunlight is more abundant. Turkish women in general, however, exhibited lower levels of vitamin D compared with Turkish men because the veil restricts their exposure to sunlight. This is yet another indicator of the strong link between sunlight exposure and vitamin D. It also suggests that diet is less effective in providing vitamin D because it is reasonable to assume that Turkish women and Turkish men have the same diet.

4.3   BONE DISEASE AND THE ROLE OF SUNLIGHT AND VITAMIN D

The relationship between hypovitaminosis D and bone frailty, especially hip fractures, among older people has been demonstrated in numerous studies (Holick, 2004). This problem has been shown to be particularly acute at the end of the winter season when days are shorter and exposure to sunlight is minimal (Webb *et al.*, 1990) and when people have had exposure to little sunlight for months. An Australian study examined the association between changes of season, incidence of hip fracture, and vitamin D levels in a population of elderly, not very mobile patients in the Tasmania region (Inderjeeth *et al.*, 2002). Of these patients, 68% either lived in institutional care or were dependent on a care-provider for mobility. Almost half of them (48%) indicated that they went outdoors less than once a week. This study found no significant seasonal variations in vitamin D concentration among these patients because most were bed-ridden or housebound and received little vitamin D from photosynthesis. Regardless of diet, they remained deficient in vitamin D and their bone frailty could not be overcome, another finding that highlights the vital importance of sunlight in the production of vitamin D and the ineffectiveness of dietary solutions.

Elderly people suffer more from vitamin D deficiency than younger populations because the ability of our skin to photosynthesize and produce vitamin D is significantly reduced as we age (MacLaughlin and Holick, 1985). Tests revealed that vitamin D production by skin photosynthesis is four times lower in people over the age of 65 than in a younger population between the ages of 20 and 30 (Holick *et al.*, 1989). If there is an architectural lesson to be learned from this it is that health care facilities, nursing homes and buildings that house elderly people should have higher requirements for sunlight and need to be designed to allow for greater access to sunlight than other types of buildings.

There are numerous scientific indications that point to the strong relationship between sunlight, or lack thereof, and vitamin D, and to the weaker link between diet and vitamin D. For example, rickets, a disease long eradicated in most developed countries, continues to be prevalent in countries where infants are swaddled and women are confined to the home or assigned a dress code that covers the body. A strong relationship between vitamin D and fetal bone development and a greater risk of bone frailty is found among residents of many northern states of the United States because of climate conditions and not because of dietary causes (Kreiter *et al.*, 2000; Weisberg *et al.*, 2004). The role of vitamin D in the regulation of calcium and phosphorous absorption and in metabolism for bone health is especially crucial during pregnancy and lactation because of the rapid development of the bones of the fetus and the newborn child. Women have less skin pigmentation than men; as a result, they need more vitamin D, especially during pregnancy.

4.4   HEART DISEASES AND THE ROLE OF SUNLIGHT AND VITAMIN D

In addition to rickets, and bone loss and fracture, inadequate vitamin D is believed to have multiple harmful effects on our cardiovascular systems. Reports suggest that when vitamin D is deficient, heart failure can result but such failure is reversible when our bodies are replenished with vitamin D (Rostand, 1997). Medical tests show that hypovitaminosis D is common among patients with heart failure, and it is responsible for several heart malfunctions such as hypertension (Shane *et al.*, 1997; Schleithoff *et al.*, 2003; Chen *et al.*, 2005). Hypertension is considered a major risk factor for heart failure. Although factors causing hypertension may be genetic, hypertension can also be caused by the environment. Epidemiological evidence links insufficiencies of vitamin D to hypertension (Rostand, 1997). Supplements of vitamin D were found to reduce systolic blood pressure in elderly women who had low vitamin D levels, while ultraviolet-B radiation was found to reduce arterial pressure in patients with mild hypertension (Krause *et al.*, 1998).

There are indications that vitamin D can help patients with kidney diseases. It can be used as a palliative measure to improve blood pressure and renal osteodystrophy, a bone disease that occurs when the kidneys fail to maintain adequate levels of calcium and phosphorus in the blood. Prasad and colleagues (2001) found seasonal patterns in blood pressure among dialysis and renal transplant patients. These patients registered higher blood pressure in winter than in summer, in all likelihood due to the difference in daylight hours that patients experienced in seasonal cycles. The longer their exposure to daylight, the more normal their blood pressure became.

4.5 MULTIPLE SCLEROSIS AND THE ROLE OF SUNLIGHT AND VITAMIN D

There are millions of people who are afflicted by multiple sclerosis (MS), one of several degenerative diseases that, like diabetes type 1 and rheumatoid arthritis, afflict millions of people. There are about 85 people with MS for every 10 000 people in the USA. It is estimated that the worldwide population with MS is around 2.5 million and that about 50% more females are afflicted with MS than males (Noonan, 2002; MS Society Statistics, 2006).

Data show that MS is more prevalent in latitudinal regions farthest away from the equator and it is believed that there is a correlation between MS and UV-B exposure (Davenport *et al.*, 1922). Davenport found that men in the armed services who grew up in Wisconsin, Michigan and the extreme US northwest had the highest MS incidence among all other men in the armed services. He also noted that men in urban areas had 50% more MS incidence than those in rural areas. He contends that reduced exposure to sunlight and UV-B in cities as a result of pollution and dense urban fabric may be the cause for such higher incidence. Two other studies following that of Davenport also suggested a strong link between sunlight and MS; one focusing on men in the armed forces (Acheson *et al.*, 1960), and the other on veterans (Norman *et al.*, 1983). Both of these studies confirmed a negative correlation between exposure to sunlight and MS incidence: that is, the higher the exposure to sunlight the lower the incidence, and *vice versa*. Figure 4.3, provided by the Sunlight Nutrition and Health

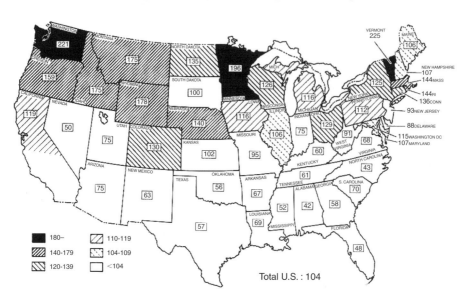

Figure 4.3 Geographical distribution of MS in the United States (http://www.sunarc.org/).

Research Center, a governmental agency of the United States, illustrates a positive correlation between latitude and MS incidence, or, in other words, a negative correlation between sunlight and MS. The figure indicates not only that there is lower incidence of multiple sclerosis in the southern states compared with the northern ones, but also higher incidence in urban and denser regions than in low density ones.

4.6 CANCER AND THE ROLE OF SUNLIGHT AND VITAMIN D

Skin cancer has many causes but UV radiation is one. The harmful effects of UV radiation may be prevented by avoiding excessive exposure to sunlight and other sources of UV radiation. This type of cancer is the type increasing most quickly in the United States and is the most commonly diagnosed malignancy, exceeding lung, breast, colon, or prostate cancer. More than one million Americans will be diagnosed with skin cancer in 2007 (American Cancer Society, 2007).

While skin cancer can be caused by UV radiation, research also suggests that sunlight, by way of vitamin D, can prevent a number of internal cancers (Grant and Garland, 2006). The number of deaths from internal cancers far exceeds the mortality rate from skin cancer, according to a publication by the American Cancer Institute (Table 4.1). The number of deaths

Table 4.1 Estimated numbers of new cases and deaths for common cancer types.

Cancer type	Estimated new cases	Estimated deaths
Bladder	67160	13750
Breast (female – male)	178480–2030	40460–450
Colon and rectal (combined)	153760	52180
Endometrial	39080	7400
Kidney (renal cell)	43512	10957
Leukemia (all)	44240	21790
Lung (including bronchus)	213380	160390
Melanoma	59940	8110
Non-Hodgkin lymphoma	63190	18660
Pancreatic	37170	33370
Prostate	218890	27050
Skin (nonmelanoma)	>1000000	<2000
Thyroid	33550	1530

in 2007 due to nonmelanoma skin cancer is estimated to be less than 2000 and the number of deaths due to melanoma cancer is about 8000; however, over 52 000 deaths from colon and rectal cancer, over 27 000 deaths from prostate cancer, and over 40 000 from breast cancer are likely to occur (American Cancer Society, 2007).

According to William Grant, Director of the Sunlight, Nutrition and Health Research Center (Sunarc) in California, excessive exposure to sunlight causes 1600 deaths a year in the United Kingdom from melanoma skin cancer. Insufficient exposure to sunlight, however, causes 25 000 deaths a year from internal cancers. According to Dr Grant, UV-B radiation was inversely correlated with 16 types of cancer for white Americans, primarily epithelial cancers of the digestive and reproductive systems. Others have also pointed to an association between vitamin D deficiency and other types of internal cancer including colon, breast, and prostate cancer (Garland and Garland, 1980; Garland et al., 1989; Gorham et al., 2005; Holick, 2006; Grant and Garland, 2006).

When examining the geographic distribution of cancer mortality rates in the United States (Figures 4.4–4.5 and 4.6) a positive correlation between latitude and three types of cancer mortality rates becomes apparent. Put differently, there is an inverse correlation between exposure to UV radiation and

Figure 4.4 Colon cancer mortality by state economic area (age-adjusted 1970 US population) among white males, 1970–1994 (courtesy of William B. Grant).

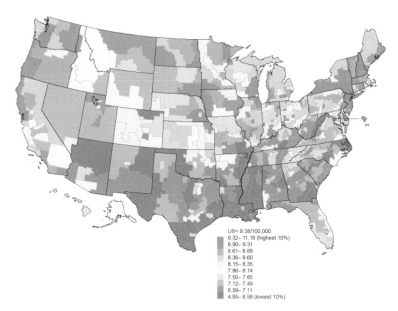

US= 8.38/100,000
9.32– 11.16 (highest 10%)
8.90– 9.31
8.61– 8.89
8.36– 8.60
8.15– 8.35
7.86– 8.14
7.50– 7.85
7.12– 7.49
6.59– 7.11
4.85– 6.58 (lowest 10%)

Figure 4.5 Ovarian cancer mortality by state economic area (age-adjusted 1970 US population) among white females, 1970–1994 (courtesy of William B. Grant).

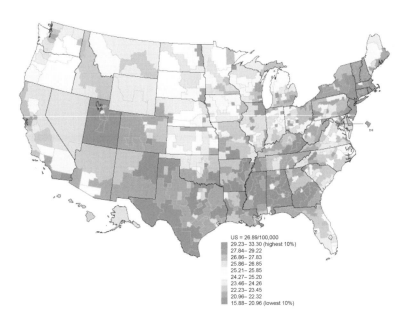

US = 26.89/100,000
29.23– 33.30 (highest 10%)
27.84– 29.22
26.86– 27.83
25.86– 26.85
25.21– 25.85
24.27– 25.20
23.46– 24.26
22.23– 23.45
20.96– 22.32
15.88– 20.96 (lowest 10%)

Figure 4.6 Breast cancer mortality by state economic area (age-adjusted 1970 US population) among white females, 1970–1994 (courtesy of William B. Grant).

rates of breast, colon, and ovarian cancer. The farther north, the less the solar radiation and the higher the rate of cancer incidence and mortality. Numerous studies have investigated these correlations and there seems to be general agreement that vitamin D gained through sunlight reduces the incidences of prostate, ovarian, and breast cancers. Table 4.2 (Heisler, 2005) summarizes the results of an extensive literature review of different types of internal cancers, the influence of UV and vitamin D, and the incidence and death rates for each type of cancer. Three types of investigations are reviewed: ecological, case study, and cohort investigations. This summary provides evidence of the strong association between sunlight and cancer. Van der Rhee and de Vries (2006) reviewed 26 publications on this subject and found an inverse correlation between sunlight exposure and mortality or incidence of three types of cancer. Eight of the 26 publications dealt with prostate cancer and each showed an inverse correlation between exposure to sunlight and prostate cancer

Table 4.2 Diseases in the United States associated in the literature with UV radiation arranged in order for US deaths per year (usually 2001). Incidence and mortality are per annum from recent years.

Disease	Incidence/100 000	US cases	US deaths	UV influence	Vitamin D influence
Colon cancer	39		53 000	RR, MRR	RR, MRR
Breast cancer	28 (F)		41 800	RR, MRR	RR
Prostate cancer	161		30 700	RR, MRR	RR (M)
Pancreas	11		29 800	RR	
Non-Hodgkin lymphoma	18		22 300	RR	
Cancer of ovary	13		14 400	RR, MRR	
Cancer of esophagus	5		12 500	RR	
Bladder cancer	21		12 200	RR	
Kidney cancer	13		12 100	RR(M)	
Multiple myeloma	5		10 700	RR	
Rectal cancer	14		8500	RR	
Melanoma	17	55 000	7900	RI, MRR	
Uterus corpus	23		3200	RR	
Squamous cell carcinoma	105		2500	High Risk	
Cataract		350 000	Occurs post surgery	UV among many suspected risk factors	
Basal cell carcinoma	475 (M), 250 (F)	900 000	rare	High risk factor	

M, male; F, female; RI, incidence risk increase; RR, risk reduction; MRR, mortality risk reduction (reproduced by permission of G. Heisler).

incidence or mortality. The level of prevention seems to be proportional to the exposure to sunlight in a 'dose–response' relationship. That is, the higher the exposure to sunlight, the lower the incidence of prostate cancer. Each of the seven studies on breast cancer included in the review showed the positive influence of exposure to sunlight in reducing the incidence or mortality from breast cancer. The evidence for ovarian cancer was small but conclusive. This review indicates convincingly that sunlight has a preventive effect on the initiation and/or progression of different types of cancer. One explanation is that exposure to solar UV-B radiation reduces the risk of cancer through the photosynthesis production of vitamin D.

Vitamin D also affects our immune system. It is widely recognized that the active vitamin D metabolite $1,25(OH)_2D$ is produced not only in the kidney as previously believed but also in other tissues including colon, prostate, skin, and osteoblasts (John et al., 1999; Chen and Holick, 2003; Welsh, 2004; Schwartz, 2005; Porojnicu et al., 2005). The vitamin D metabolite produced outside the kidneys regulates various cellular functions in specific tissues, including cell growth, thereby boosting immunity against cancer growth.

Cancer and the melatonin hypothesis

Scientists have determined that low melatonin levels augment the incidence of cancer among rats (Blask et al., 1999, 2005) and some researchers have championed the causal relationship between light and some forms of cancers through what is called the melatonin hypothesis. Melatonin is produced at night or in a light-free environment. When melatonin is suppressed, it increases the production of estrogens in the ovaries, which in turn stimulate the production of breast epithelial stem cells known to increase the likelihood of breast cancer (Cohen et al., 1978).

Light exercises a major influence on melatonin and serotonin production and consequently on our circadian rhythm. Scientists speculate that the disturbance of the circadian rhythm could contribute in a major way to the cause of breast cancer (Hrushesky, 1985, 2001; Stevens, 2005). According to Reiter and colleagues (1997, 1999), melatonin can prevent DNA damage; damaged DNA can mutate and trigger the production of cancerous cells. The evidence that relates circadian rhythm disturbance and melatonin suppression to the presence of light at night (LAN) to the incidence of cancer is demonstrated in night shift workers. Approximately 8 million workers in the United States regularly work at night, and for many of these individuals (e.g., nurses, security personnel, physicians, and airline pilots) peak alertness and maximum performance are critical. In addition to performance issues, Horowitz and colleagues (2001) found that night shift nurses not only experience loss of sleep and misalignment of the circadian rhythm but also suffer greater risk of gastric and duodenal ulcers and cardiovascular diseases. The timing of their sleep–wake schedule remained permanently out of phase with the natural light/dark cycle, and resulted in health problems. Lack of sufficient sleep or sleep disorders seem to make the immune system vulnerable to attack and less able to fight off potentially cancerous cells. Another survey (Schernhammer et al., 2001) showed that night shift workers are more likely to have cancer because of the LAN phenomenon, which suppresses the production of melatonin.

According to news reports, The International Agency for Research on Cancer, the cancer arm of the World Health Organization (WHO), has added overnight shift work as a probable carcinogen in December 2007. Scientists at the WHO suspect that overnight work is dangerous because it disrupts the circadian rhythm. Millions of people worldwide could be affected by this ruling because experts estimate that nearly 20% of the work force in developed countries work at night. Some day shift workers, however, also have disturbed circadian rhythm because of insufficient exposure to daylight at their workplace during the day. In September 2006, The National Institute of Environmental Health Sciences (NIEHS) convened a workshop to examine how best to conduct research on possible connections between lighting and health (Stevens, 2007). Their report outlines three major areas of future research; among them is the effect of light-induced physiologic disruption on disease occurrence and prognosis. The potential disruption of the circadian cycle, particularly at night but possibly also during the day and its contribution to the causes of cancer or other diseases is a pertinent question. The question is particularly important in part because a large and increasing segment of the population of industrialized nations is working the graveyard shift (Rajaratnam and Arendt, 2001). It is equally significant because secretion of melatonin during the night is being disturbed as a result of the population of industrialized countries reducing its exposure to darkness, as reflected in a decrease in the average duration of sleep in recent times (National Sleep Foundation 2005), and secretion of serotonin is being disturbed by insufficient exposure to daylight during the day, especially at the workplace. The combination of these two phenomena, caused by the combination of lifestyles and ill-conceived architecture, could cause circadian imbalances and serious health problems.

4.7   SUNLIGHT AND DIABETES

Diabetes is a chronic metabolism disorder characterized by hyperglycemia (high blood sugar). The World Health Organization recognizes two main forms of diabetes: type-one and type-two; and a third that can occur during pregnancy (gestational diabetes). In type-one diabetes, injection of insulin is mandatory because the beta cells of the pancreas produce no insulin, a hormone that moves the sugar from the blood to the cells. In the case of type-two diabetes, insulin may or may not be needed.

Sunlight has a direct effect on insulin secretion. Exposure to UV-B radiation has been shown to increase insulin secretion among adults (Colas *et al.*, 1988). Similarly, lower levels of blood sugar (therefore higher insulin secretion) were observed during summer (Ishii *et al.*, 2001). The Colas and Ishii studies dealt with sunlight and relationship to type-two diabetes. Other studies, however, examined the relationship between vitamin D and diabetes. The insulin-producing cells in the pancreas have vitamin D receptors and seem to function better in the presence of high vitamin D levels (Brown *et al.*, 1999). According to Chui (2004), vitamin D increases the action of insulin, which in turn increases the control of carbohydrates (sugar) in the blood. As a result, a negative correlation was found between blood sugar level and vitamin D levels.

Another study examined the effect of vitamin D supplementation on diabetic women. It showed that a daily intake of 1332 IU over a period of one month resulted in a 21.4% drop in insulin resistance and a 43.3% increase in insulin production (Borisova, 2003). It is important to note that sunlight can produce up to 20 000 IU of vitamin D per day, which can lead to enormous benefits for both type-one and type-two diabetic patients (Sorenson, 2006).

4.8   WINDOWS AND STRESS

The lack of windows in the workplace contributes to stress on the job (Heerwagen *et al.*, 1995). A recent Turkish study (Alimoglu and Donmez, 2005) investigated whether the lack of daylight in the work setting can be a predictor of job burnout of nurses who, as a group, generally have an above-average risk for work stress and burnout. Of a sample of 141 female nurses in a Turkish hospital, 46.8% reported that they were exposed to less than 3 hours of daylight during a typical work day. Using the Maslach Burnout Inventory (Maslach and Jackson, 1996) and the Work Related Strain Inventory (Revicki *et al.*, 1991) to measure burnout and stress, the study found that daylight had an indirect statistical correlation with burnout. A minimum of 3 hours of exposure to daylight seemed to reduce stress and burnout; however, the study did not specify the extent of the reduction. Roseman and Booker (1995) found that medical errors among nurses were more likely in midwinter than in the fall or summer. They reported a strong relationship between outside darkness and the rate of medical errors; however, whether the causes of such errors are psychological or are related to stress and burnout remains unclear.

4.9 HEALTH AND SPECTRAL QUALITY OF LIGHT

The spectral composition of light refers to how much of each wavelength of the visible spectrum, which ranges from 380 nm to 770 nm, a particular light source emits. Figures 4.7 and 4.8 provide a comparison of the spectral compositions of a standard 'cool white' fluorescent light source and daylight. Spectral quality is a complex term that mainly refers to how warm or cool a light appears (correlated color temperature of light, CCT) and the shift of color (Color Rendering Index, CRI) that it may cause. The CCT scale is a color-defining scale developed by William Kelvin in the late 1800s. It indicates the specific hue of a light source. The Color Rendering Index relies on a scale from 0 to 100 that represents how closely a light source depicts or reflects an object's true color. As a general rule,

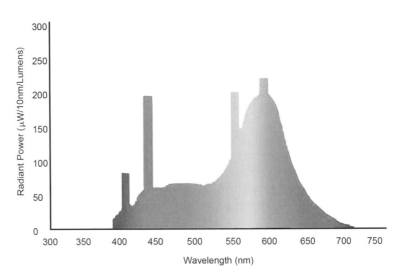

Figure 4.7 Spectral distribution of a standard 'cool white' fluorescent lamp.

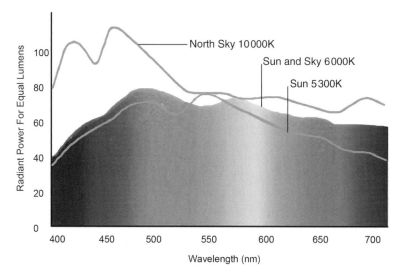

Figure 4.8 Spectral compositions of daylight.

the higher the CRI, the more accurate the color of an object will appear. Because daylight is dynamic, its color properties change. For example, a cloudy day would have a CCT ranging between 8000 and 10000 K whereas a clear northern sky at noon would have a CCT ranging from 5000 to 5500 K. In terms of its spectral composition, daylight contains 4.6% UV radiation, 46.4% visible light, and 49% infrared radiation.

The benefits of daylight in terms of its spectral qualities can best be demonstrated by the outcome of research not only on daylight but also on full spectrum lighting sources that attempt to mimic the spectral qualities of daylight. There appears to be a relationship between the spectral quality of light and the transformation of vitamin D in the skin. Bunker and Harris (1937) established that a wavelength of 297 nm is most effective in curing rickets. Knudsen and Benford (1938) found that 280 nm was the most effective in curing rickets and that wavelengths of 265, 289, 302, and 312 nm also had anti-rickets effects. Wavelengths longer than 312 nm had no effects on rickets.

Researchers in the United States Environmental Protection Agency (EPA) investigated the relative mutagenic (capable of causing mutations) effects of sunlight, fluorescent light, and typical tanning bed light on the DNA of *Salmonella typhimurium*, a laboratory bacterium often used for preliminary investigations in biomedical research (De Marini *et al.*, 1995). In this experiment researchers exposed four strains of this bacterium to sunlight, cool white fluorescent light, and tanning bed light for the same amount of time. The total radiant exposure received by each set of cultures was reported as the sum of the individual exposures to UV-A (315–400 nm), UV-B (280–315 nm), UV-C (250–280 nm) and the rest of the visible spectrum (400–800 nm). In every case, the cultures exposed to sunlight received the highest amount of radiation; however, the relative amount of UV-A and UV-B exposure varied by light type. Tanning light had a 2:1 constant ratio of UV-A to UV-B, cool white fluorescent light had a ratio of 10:1, for sunlight the ratio was 50:1.

Compared with an irradiated control group, all strains exhibited transformation of the genetic information (DNA). Tanning light, containing 80% of UV light, spurred more mutations than sunlight or cool white fluorescent light which contained no more than 10% of UV light. This experiment shows that the ability to cause mutation (mutagenicity) is strongly dependent on both the total amount of UV radiation contained in the light spectrum and the relative amount of UV-B versus UV-A within that spectrum. These results, though not conclusive, indicate that it is the nature of the light spectrum in sunlight that makes it a unique enhancement to human health. Most electric light sources do not replicate the sunlight spectrum. Furthermore, the spectral composition of sunlight changes according to the time of day and the season. This changing cycle may be the central reason for human circadian rhythms, assuming that chemical reactions to promote or inhibit alertness are initiated by UV levels contained in daylight.

Other health benefits of sunlight are found in its effect on liver metabolite, a substance produced by the liver that acts on our metabolism. Exposure to natural light stimulates the secretion of liver metabolite (Neer *et al.*, 1977), but artificially simulated daylight that mimics the spectral composition of daylight also seems to have positive health benefits. Neer's research indicated that increases in the absorption of intestinal calcium were found among healthy men kept indoors during the winter and exposed to high intensity levels of artificially simulated daylight reaching 5000 lux, a level much above that typically found in building interiors using electrical lighting.

4.10   HOW MUCH VITAMIN D IS NEEDED?

According to several sources (Sardar *et al.*, 1996; Glorieux and Feldman, 1997; Holick, 1999), the need for vitamin D photosynthesis can range from 15 minutes a day, three or four times a week, to three hours a day, three or four times a week. The length of exposure depends on the type of skin, the season, and the geographic location. Fifteen minutes of sunlight will produce enough Vitamin D to last for several days, even when the subject is wearing light clothing; however, three or more hours are required to produce enough vitamin D for dark-skinned people. Michael Holick (2004) from Boston University, author of the *UV Advantage* web-based information program (www.uvadvantage.org), estimates that we need to expose 25% of our bodies to midday solar radiation, two or thee times a week during summer to produce the amount of vitamin D deemed optimal.

In the United Kingdom, children from immigrant families are especially prone to rickets because it takes up to six times longer for dark skin to generate vitamin D than it does for white skin (Serhan *et al.*, 1999).

In Australia and New Zealand, short daily exposures of the arms, hands, and face to sunlight are recommended (Cancer Council Australia, 2005). Recommendations vary from five to seven minutes during midday periods in the summer in the sunniest northern parts of Australia to 40 minutes during the midday winter hours in New Zealand.

The World Health Organization has responsibility for defining the 'International Unit' (IU) of vitamin D. One IU of vitamin D is equal to 0.025 micrograms, which is also equivalent to 65.0 pmoles. An outside exposure of hands, arms, and face for 10 to 20 minutes three times a week produces 200 to 400 IU of vitamin D during the summer months. Estimates suggest that 100 to 200 IU of vitamin D are produced for each 5% of body surface exposed.

The vitamin D requirement for healthy adults has never been precisely defined. Since vitamin D is produced in the skin after exposure to sunlight, we do not have an additional need for vitamin D when sufficient sunlight is available; however, vitamin D does become an important nutritional factor in the absence of sunlight. Nonetheless, the current recommended dietary allowance (RDA) of vitamin D in 1989 by the Food and Nutrition Board of the Commission on Life Sciences of the National Research Council is currently 5 µg/day or 200 IU for populations up to the age of 50, 10 µg/day (400 IU) for those between the age of 51 and 70, and 15 µg/day (600 IU) for those 70 years old or older. Many researchers, however, estimate that this requirement should be much higher. Even with this possibly low RDA, most healthy individuals living in the United States are deficient in vitamin D (Fuller, 2003). Evidence suggests that the daily intake of vitamin D for people with limited exposure to sunlight should be 20–25 µg (800–1000 IU) (Glerup *et al.*, 2000). In addition, because we use vitamin D less efficiently as we age, optimum intake of vitamin D must increase with age.

The typical recommendations for optimal exposure to sunlight for vitamin D production are intended for outdoor exposure. Because glass filters out about 95% of the UV-B rays, recommendations for indoor exposure need to be about nine to ten times higher than those for outdoor exposure.

4.11   DIETARY SUPPLEMENTS

The debate about whether sunlight is more effective than dietary supplements in the production of vitamin D has been examined in two studies, one in the United States and the other in Sweden. The American study (Webb *et al.*, 1990) found that seasonal variations in serum 25(OH)D concentrations (vitamin D) caused by exposure to sunlight were highest in subjects with high mobility and declined substantially and proportionally as subjects became less mobile, irrespective of vitamin D dietary supplements. The Swedish investigation (Landin-Wilhelmsen *et al.*, 1995) confirmed these findings. The Swedish researchers concluded that although helpful, dietary supplements could not supplant entirely the effects of sunlight on vitamin D levels and that adequate measures must be taken to guarantee access to sunlight, especially for those who may be less mobile or have minimal outdoor activity.

4.12   CANCER AND URBAN DENSITY

A study that compared women living and working in London with those living outside the city, found that city-dwelling women were more likely than their rural peers to have dense breasts (Gordon, 2007). A report of cancer incidence data from 1968 to 1972 for cities of different sizes and levels of urbanization in New York state, excluding New York city, was published in the *American Journal of Epidemiology* (Nasca *et al.*, 1980). It indicated a direct association between population density and cancer incidence. A significant linear association between cancer incidence and population density was observed among males and females for cancers of the buccal cavity and pharynx, the esophagus, bronchus and lung, stomach and colon. The report noted that for carcinomas of the liver, gallbladder, pancreas, bladder, larynx, and rectum, this association was observed only among males. For malignant neoplasms of the brain and nervous system, only females demonstrated a statistically significant relationship between these two variables.

When we examine internal cancer mortality rates (Figures 4.4, 4.5 and 4.6) and consider the degree of urbanization in the United States (Figure 4.9), the markedly higher rates of

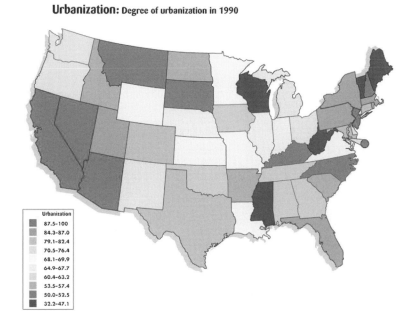

Urbanization: Degree of urbanization in 1990

Urbanization
- 87.5-100
- 84.3-87.0
- 79.1-82.4
- 70.5-76.4
- 68.1-69.9
- 64.9-67.7
- 60.4-63.2
- 53.5-57.4
- 50.0-52.5
- 32.2-47.1

Figure 4.9 Geographical distribution of the degree of urbanization in the United States (courtesy William B. Grant).

invasive cancers in urban areas are readily apparent compared with the mortality rate in rural areas. According to Grant (2004), seven types of internal cancer were found to be inversely correlated with both solar UV-B radiation and rural residence, a finding that suggests that urban residence reduces UV-B exposure and, consequently, increases cancer incidence.

When we consider latitude and urban density and their effect on the incidence of cancer, it is reasonable to assume that the lack of sunlight, and consequently of UV radiation, is an important cause of cancer. Space planning policies and poorly designed buildings that do not allow adequate sunlight should be considered agents of ill health just as any other toxic agent.

In conclusion, and if we accept that insufficient daylight in our everyday lives disturbs our circadian rhythm, then a number of population groups are at risk for illnesses such as cancer. One population group that falls into this category includes those living and/or working in high-density urban settings. In the previous chapter we noted that light levels averaging between 2500 and 10 000 lux are needed if bright light therapy is to affect mood and overcome depression. The strong connection between mood, depression, circadian rhythm, and the hormonal balance in our bodies suggests

Figure 4.10 Light level disparity between levels found at the top
of a building and those found at street level in Manhattan, New York
(courtesy of Jay Davidson).

that therapeutic levels of light are necessary for healthy
functioning, but these levels are neither attained inside our
buildings if we rely only on electric lighting nor are they
available in some populated urban centers such as New
York City. Daylight levels on a street in one of the canyons in
Manhattan, New York, have been as low as 1200 lux, 1/100th
of the 120000 lux measured on the roof top of an adjacent
building on a clear sunny day (Figure 4.10). Of the daylight
found at street level, only a small percentage (perhaps 2%
or less) will penetrate adjacent buildings. Within such high

density urban settings, some residents live in sub-basement apartments, others work in basement or sub-basement stores and factories, and still others may have limited mobility because of illnesses or advanced age. People in these groups may not receive adequate amounts of daylight and their health may be at risk. Furthermore, interior light levels in most buildings are usually far below levels deemed therapeutic. Because of utility costs and environmental concerns, we cannot rely on electric lighting to supply therapeutic levels of illumination.

Psychology of lighting

5

Because we are dependent on light for perception, it is natural that we should be psychologically affected by it. Throughout our history we have attached metaphysical, even divine, qualities to light. Light plays a central role in our everyday lives and consciousness through the physiological processes that connect our health to it. We wonder at the beauty of a sunrise or sunset with its ever-changing colors. Sunlight gives us a sense of time and a connection with the outside world, a connection often needed by our inner biological clock.

The history of architecture is one of a relationship between ourselves and sunlight. Light is often used by architects as a metaphor, a mood-giver or a carrier of a meaning in and of itself. The works of past and present master architects express this central role. Much of their work is highly acclaimed because of the magnificent interplay between structure, form, and light. The chapel of Notre-Dame-du-Haut at Ronchamp, France, by Le Corbusier is a boldly expressive free-form structure in which the symbiotic association between the form and the interior natural light identifies the essence of the building, making it the central element of the design concept. Through irregularly sized and shaped windows piercing the southern thick masonry wall of the chapel (Figure 5.1) and from three light towers emerging through the roof much like wind catchers (Figures 5.2 and 5.3), light enters the space from multiple directions, bouncing off richly

Figure 5.1 Notre-Dame-du-Haut chapel, Ronchamp, France, Le Corbusier, 1950–1954.

Figure 5.2 Light tower at the Notre-Dame-du-Haut Chapel, Ronchamp, France (courtesy of James P. Warfield).

textured surfaces, and through colored glass that imparts unequalled poetic and spiritual qualities that have made the building one of the icons of modern architecture.

In the Chapel of Light by the Japanese architect Tadao Ando in Osaka, Japan (Figures 5.4 and 5.5), light enters from

Figure 5.3   Light tower at the Notre-Dame-du-Haut Chapel, Ronchamp, France.

behind the altar through a cruciform cut in the concrete wall that extends vertically from floor to ceiling. Light emerges through the crucifix as an abstract and universal event in contrast to the darkness of the concrete wall. The effortless simplicity of the space is contrasted only by the intense brightness of the luminous crucifix, making it the centerpiece of the chapel and of the spiritual experience sought by those who frequent it.

In architect Fay Jones's Mildred B. Cooper Memorial Chapel in the Ozarks of the United States, and like his much-celebrated Thorncrown chapel, light wraps the entire chapel and its occupants. As sunlight enters the chapel, it is filtered by the tall trees and the 6000 square feet of glass that is supported by an exquisite and elaborate structure of wooden columns and pine wood trusses (Figures 5.6 and 5.7). The end result is a chapel of light where the natural and the man-made fuse and become one.

5.1   LIGHT AND MOOD

Initial studies exploring lighting and human behavior focused on our preferences in lighting conditions, particularly in the workplace. The common results among these studies suggest that people prefer much higher light levels

Figure 5.4   Tadao's Chapel of Light in Osaka, Japan (courtesy of Tadao Ando Architects).

than those typically recommended by professional organizations such as the Illuminating Engineering Society in North America (IESNA) or the Chartered Institution of Building Services Engineers (CIBSE) in the United Kingdom. To cite only a few examples, American students were found to prefer illuminance levels as much as three times higher than those recommended (Leslie and Hartleb, 1990). Office workers performing clerical work preferred light levels 50%

Figure 5.5   Tadao's Chapel of Light in Osaka, Japan (courtesy of Tadao Ando Architects).

higher than those generally recommended (500 lux) according to two studies in the United States (Hughes and McNelis, 1978; Barnaby, 1980). A Dutch study found that office workers would prefer to have on average 800 lux more than was supplied by their electric lighting system, regardless of the amount of daylight available (Aarts, 1994). A similar result was found for British office workers (Saunders, 1969). The consensus findings of these studies are not surprising since

Figure 5.6   Central aisle of the Fay Jones's Mildred B. Cooper Memorial Chapel (courtesy of Angel Valtiera).

most of the lighting recommendations made by professional organizations are intended to be minimum light levels, with the expectation that actual levels would be higher.

Realizing the significance of the impact of light on architecture, researchers began exploring the relationship between light and the mood of the building occupants. Not only in sacred or religious places but also in social places such as restaurants, theaters, and opera houses do we experience mood changes manipulated by dramatic lighting. In places where lighting is not so dramatic, such as an office building or other workplaces, mood changes because of lighting may

Figure 5.7 Roof structure of the Fay Jones's Mildred B. Cooper Memorial Chapel (courtesy of Angel Valtiera).

be more subtle and not as clearly discernable. Environmental psychologists and behaviorists assert that even in less dramatic luminous conditions, small changes in lighting can alter the mood and the emotional state of the building occupants (Flynn, 1977; Beltcher and Kluczny, 1987). The general paradigm underlying this premise is that the presence or absence of light, along with other environmental stimuli, can produce a positive or a negative effect. The sensations that accompany good lighting include excitement, alertness, and dominance. In contrast, poor lighting results in dullness, boredom, and submissiveness. The paradigm posits further that these affective states in turn mediate the social behavioral response of the occupants of the room and the decision making in a workplace environment (Mehrabian and Russell, 1974).

Evidence suggests that light affects mood and that mood influences or mediates the problem-solving process that people use at work (Isen *et al.*, 1982). When people are upbeat and in a good mood, they perform better and *vice versa*. The meaning of mood as used by environmental psychologists studying lighting and other environmental attributes refers to the short-term meaning of mood (Russell and Snodgrass, 1987). In other words, it is not the overt reaction that would follow a direct stimulus but rather the internal experience of the person that occurs as a result of a stimulus such as light intensity or color or scenery, which touches our senses and in turn gives rise to a behavioral reaction (Hesselgren, 1975).

Some of the key ingredients of lighting are how much light is present (illuminance), and the quality of that light, mainly characterized by its spectral quality. Lighting conditions that produce positive effects influence cognitive task performance and social behaviors (Baron *et al.*, 1992). Baron's study showed a general association between lighting and mood; however, it could not confirm the assumption that the greater the illuminance, the better the mood.

In an attempt to investigate how designers can assess the impact of sunlight on office workers and measure that impact on their mood and affective response, Boubekri and colleagues (1991) addressed the issue of sunlight penetration, not in terms of light levels but in a rather novel and unique way. The ratio between the size of the sun patches in a room to the total floor area of the room was used as an independent variable to assess the impact of sunlight on the affective response of the office occupants (Figure 5.8). This study found that a moderate amount of sunlight penetration (between 25% and 40%) was optimal for generating a feeling of excitement and cheerfulness among office workers in an air conditioned room. Sunlight penetration above 40% was perceived negatively by the office occupants.

In an experiment involving electric lighting, Beltcher and Kluczny (1987) examined the effect of illuminance levels

Figure 5.8 Sunlight penetration measured as the ratio between the area of the sun patch to the area of the entire room (photograph: M. Boubekri).

and color temperature of light from electric light sources on mood and decision making in an office situation, while simultaneously exploring probable differences between the responses of men and women. Their study revealed that different lighting conditions do in fact trigger different mood responses and, consequently, affect the decisions made by the workers. The mood of female participants shifted in response to different light levels in an opposite direction to that of men as hypothesized by the investigators. The mood swing of women was strongly negative under bright light conditions and near zero under dim conditions. Interestingly, men tended to respond in the opposite fashion. Women applied more rigorous decision making under high illumination than under lower illumination, but the phenomenon was reversed for men who applied more rigorous thinking and decision making under dim light. Such findings could seriously impact the way workplaces are designed to meet preference differences based on gender.

Other studies have also revealed differences between men and women in the way they are affected by their environment or in the way they perceive it. A post-occupancy evaluation of an office building in Montreal, Canada (Boubekri and Haghighat, 1993) indicated that mean scores of overall satisfaction with lighting were found to be consistently higher among men than among women working under the same conditions, implying that women tend to be more critical of or are more sensitive to their luminous environment than are men. Men apparently pay less attention to the condition of their workplace. Critics, however, suggest that many of the lighting ergonomics studies have flaws and may contain procedural, perhaps even fundamental, mistakes and should be taken with some caution (Veitch and Newsham, 1996). Inconsistencies among studies of how lighting affects our moods and emotional states have also been found. Nevertheless, sufficient evidence indicates a causal relationship between the two, and experts need to clarify what that relationship is in order to design spaces with the comfort and well-being of occupants in mind.

The majority of research exploring the relationship between light and mood has largely focused on electric lighting. The initial interest in daylighting occurred in the 1960s and 1970s, primarily in an attempt to reduce energy consumption in buildings and the reliance on fossil fuels. Initial behavioral studies pertaining to daylighting focused on whether daylight was preferred to electric light and the degree of that preference, if any. Pioneers in the field of the psychology of lighting such as Gibson (1971), Flynn (1977), and others focused primarily on electric lighting, although some of the results of their work can be applied to daylighting. Gibson first introduced the concept of *lighting structure* in the early 1970s, equating it to a physical entity. According to him, '*light ought not to be considered merely as a stimulus to our senses but also as a structure that can convey information.*' Light as a structuring element in a room can influence our perception of a space, including spatial comprehension, path selection and orientation, and social interaction. It also may affect worker arousal, motivation, and performance.

Unlike electric lighting where the properties are static, the dynamic and constantly changing aspect of daylight, though interesting from a psychological point of view, has made daylighting a difficult field of study. The changing character of daylight from one minute to the next makes experimental investigations difficult because of concern over conditions of validity and of replication.

The importance of daylight in our lives can be seen, however, in the marketing strategies of lamp manufacturers and in the push for full-spectrum fluorescent fixtures as surrogates for daylighting, even though these lamps tend to cost considerably more than equivalent standard fluorescent ones. The hypothesis favoring full spectrum light is based on the assumption that electric light approximating daylight in its spectral composition is naturally better for human beings. This argument has been put forward as the 'evolutionary hypothesis' (McColl and Veitch, 2001), which states that human beings respond better to the perennial natural environment under which they evolved than to an ephemeral, man-made one. Although widely accepted, this theory remains untested.

This general innate preference for daylight could be related to the spectral qualities of daylight and to its dynamic character that trigger hormonal and physiological processes, which, in turn, affect our psychological well-being. Whatever the explanation, the fact remains that most people prefer natural lighting and feel better under daylit conditions than under artificial lighting.

5.2 THE PSYCHOLOGY OF DAYLIGHTING AND WINDOWS

Daylight is inextricably linked to windows and openings within the exterior envelope of a building. The two cannot be separated under typical design approaches, although it is technologically possible to bring in daylight without windows through the use of light pipes and other strategies.

Figure 5.9 Sunlight brought into an underground office 30 meters below ground on the campus of the University of Minnesota (photograph: M. Boubekri).

Figure 5.9 illustrates a case where sunlight is brought into an underground research office, located about 100 feet below ground on the campus of the University of Minnesota, using a light pipe system. This system relies on a mirror located on the top of the roof and housed within a glass box (Figure 5.10). The mirror sends light to the underground space through a simple shaft opening within the building.

The idea that people prefer to live and work in buildings that have windows is generally well accepted and widely documented. The benefits of windows were demonstrated in a study in Washington, DC by the Center for Building Performance of the US Department of Energy (Hartkopf *et al.*, 1994). On average, major health complaints were between 20% and 25% lower for persons close to an exterior window compared with those who worked in the interior core, without access to view and daylight. People often add skylights to their homes just to have more natural light because it makes them feel better. Windows play several roles and have more than one effect on a room and its occupants. The changing character of daylight adds a dynamic qualitative dimension to the ambiance of the room that is not easily achievable with an electric illuminant. Windows allow diffuse daylight and sunlight inside a room while providing views to the outside, thereby adding a sense of openness, spaciousness, and orientation. Because of the technological advances of the last five decades, we are able to design buildings with large glass façades that permit daylight to enter and allow

Figure 5.10   Mirror collecting sunlight and sending it to an underground office 30 meters below ground on the campus of the University of Minnesota (photograph: M. Boubekri).

views to the outside. On the other hand, these same technological advances gave rise to long-spanning structural systems and large floor plates that pushed many workstations towards the inner core of the building and away from the exterior walls. Even with glass curtain walls many employees are located far from the peripheral walls with neither the daylight nor the views. Even buildings with many windows house workers who do not benefit from these amenities (Figure 5.11). The importance of the connection with the outside world can be observed in the behavior of people

Figure 5.11 An office building in Montreal, Canada, with windows but where most workers don't have access to views to the outside (photograph: M. Boubekri).

who live and work in windowless spaces. They appear to use twice as many visual materials to decorate their workstations than do their counterparts who have windows. Landscape scenes and nature-related themes seem to be the prevalent content of these visuals, an indication of a need to connect with the natural world (Heerwagen and Orians, 1986). Dissatisfaction levels run very high among 90% of workers in windowless offices. About half of the employees surveyed felt that windowless environments affected them and their work negatively (Ruys, 1971).

Some countries have assumed a forward thinking, pro-user approach by recognizing the importance of windows. The Netherlands, for example, now requires that buildings be designed so that all occupants are no more than 27 feet from a window. In the majority of countries, however, daylight and views take a back seat to other considerations such as economy. For most building codes worldwide, the function of windows is to allow smoke to be vented out in case of fire and to provide escape routes for people in case of emergencies, rather than to bring in natural light. Almost all building codes do not require windows to bring in a certain level of daylight into the building.

The minimum size of a window needed to fulfill satisfactorily a connection with the outside world has been the subject of a major study in the United Kingdom (Ne'eman and Hopkinson, 1970; Ne'eman and Longmore, 1973). These

Figure 5.12   A small window provides little information about close objects (photograph: M. Boubekri).

researchers found that a window 11 feet in width would satisfy 85% of the room occupants. No mention was made about window height, however. The deciding factor for what should be the minimum size did not seem to be dictated by the luminance (or brightness) of the window or by how much daylight it allowed in if the room had sufficient electric light, which was the case in this experiment. The amount of visual information contained in the view appeared to be the most significant factor. The important criteria seemed to be whether the visual information the window provided was intelligible and how complete the information about the world outside was. A window that was too small to provide complete visual information was much less desirable. Near objects, such as buildings, required larger windows than did distant objects (Figures 5.12 and 5.13). Attention to the outside world proved an important ingredient to relieve a sense of enclosure.

5.3   PSYCHOLOGY OF LIGHT AND PRODUCTIVITY

Environmental designers have been interested in the relationship between lighting and job performance since the early studies by Elton Mayo (1933) at The Western Electric Hawthorne Works in Chicago, where he examined productivity and work conditions, especially lighting. A resurgence of

Figure 5.13   A large window provides more information about close objects (photograph: M. Boubekri).

interest in the study of natural lighting and building fenestration design has occurred over the last four decades because of the effect of daylight on job performance and worker well-being (Boubekri and Haghighat, 1993). To what extent light affects the psychological well-being of people in addition to their visual performance has been the key question. Researchers agree that visual performance and user satisfaction are enhanced with increased illuminance up to a point (Weston, 1949; Blackwell, 1959; Hopkinson *et al.*, 1966; Boyce, 1973). An assertion, yet to be proven, stipulates that for the same visual tasks, people require 20% less illuminance under daylight than under electric light. This difference is attributed to such superior attributes of daylight as its dynamic character and full spectral distribution. Studies also reported that because of these same qualities the tolerance of viewers to visual discomfort coming from daylighting tends to be higher than that from electric light sources (Figure 5.14). For instance, the Daylight Glare Index differs from the glare

Figure 5.14   The tolerance of viewers for visual discomfort coming from daylighting tends to be higher than that from electric light sources (photograph: M. Boubekri).

index from electric light sources not only because daylight sources tend to be large and require different quantification methods but also because the level of tolerance for daylighting glare is higher than that for electric lighting (Chauvel and Dogniaux, 1982; Boubekri and Boyer, 1992).

Physical and environmental attributes of the workplace such as views, daylight, acoustics, and privacy are important design considerations and have been the subject of many post-occupancy evaluations. Issues of daylight and views are almost always at the very top of lists of important attributes workers would like at their workplaces. Markus (1967) found this to be the case in a survey of 400 employees in an office building in the United Kingdom, where windows were deemed extremely important because *'they supplied sunlight and a view to the outside.'* Another survey of 162 workers in a renovated office building in St Louis, Missouri, also found that workers attached considerable importance to daylight and views, ranking them among the most essential attributes of the workplace (Ne'eman *et al.*, 1984). Research suggests, however, that satisfaction with any environmental or physical attribute of the workplace and its importance rating by workers depends on the state of that attribute. Workers who are the least satisfied with an attribute, or those who don't have it at all, tend to consider it important. Those who are most satisfied with it might take it for granted and not attach as much importance to it as other workers who may have less of that attribute (Hopkinson, 1965; Ne'eman *et al.*, 1984; Boubekri and Haghighat, 1993). In other words, workers who are least satisfied with a given feature of their workplace, for example the absence of windows or bad lighting, would consider that feature important and *vice versa*. These results support the contention that people in general are not sensitive to their visual environment unless it is lacking or in poor condition. People may not notice their lighting, thermal, or acoustical conditions unless these conditions are poor. Environmental assessments, therefore, need to take this into consideration in post-occupancy evaluations and surveys.

The General Service Administration, a federal US agency, agrees that *'since people are the most important resource and the greatest expense of any organization, the long-term cost benefits of a properly designed, user-friendly work environment should be factored into any initial cost consideration.'* The life-cycle cost of a workplace is $200 (1999 year dollar) per square foot per year for salaries, $20 per square foot per year for amortized bricks and mortar costs, and $2.00 per square foot per year for energy. As a result, a 1% productivity saving can offset a company's entire annual energy cost (Figure 5.15).

Anecdotal evidence suggests that windows, and daylight in particular, make a positive contribution to employee well-being and performance. Lockheed Corporation moved 2700 employees to a new 600 000 square foot facility that strongly emphasized the use of daylighting (Thayer, 1995). In addition to the $500 000 a year energy savings achieved after the company moved, productivity increased by 15% and employees were absent from work on 15% fewer days than previously. The estimated $2 million savings resulting from greater productivity paid for the cost of adding daylighting features after just one year.

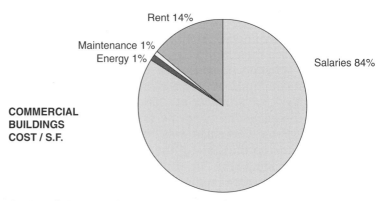

Human Productivity Improvements
Linked to Daylighting*

*Based on two fields studies – one in schools and one in retail. H.M.G. 1999

Figure 5.15　Life-cycle distribution of various building-related costs over a 40-year life of an office building. A 1% productivity saving (salaries) can nearly offset a company's entire annual energy cost.

The VeriFone Company in Los Angeles, California, reported that after their employees moved to a newly designed distribution center where extreme care was devoted to daylighting, productivity increased by 5% and total product output increased by 25% in just one and a half years after the move. The company also reported that absenteeism declined by 6.8 hours per person per year (Romm, 1999).

The NMB Bank Headquarters in The Netherlands was designed by architect Ton Alberts of Alberts and Van Huut to rely heavily on daylight. No desk could be more than 23 feet from a window. Window louvers bounce daylight deep into the space. Inside the bank, light is brought from one area into another through windows in interior walls, thereby giving all workers access to daylight, even when they are located in interior spaces. The bank has seen a significant drop in absenteeism, which is attributed to the attractive work environment (Browning, 1992).

In June 1993, a prototype Wal-Mart store, called the Eco-Mart, opened in Lawrence, Kansas. According to the company, the building was an experiment in sustainable design. The primary goal was energy efficiency. Among many energy efficiency features that the building employed (for example, a heating and cooling system that used ice storage), it utilized a special type of roof monitor as daylighting devices. According to Wal-Mart, sales per square foot were significantly higher for those departments located in the daylit half of the store and were higher than sales in the same departments in other stores that did not incorporate such daylighting features (*The Wall Street Journal*, 1995; Romm, 1999).

In another study, sales performance in 108 stores in California were compared. Two-thirds had daylighting, one-third did not. Monthly gross sales per store were averaged over an 18-month period and compared (Heschong Mahone Group, 1999a). Statistical analyses were used to control the influence of variables other than daylighting, such as number of hours open per week, population of the zip code area, average income, and number of years since a store had been remodeled. Sales rose by an average of 40% because of the use of skylights (Romm, 1999).

5.4   LIGHT AND THE SCHOOL ENVIRONMENT

Schools are another type of building that received the attention of ergonomists and where the contribution of daylighting could be verifiably demonstrated. The architecture of school buildings can shape the way we teach and learn. In the five years between 2002 and 2007, more than 1000 schools were built each year in order to meet the demand of students in kindergarten and elementary schools in the United States alone. Architects and lighting ergonomists have taken a keen interest in the learning environment, particularly in the way children are affected by the natural and electric lighting conditions under which they study.

As a surrogate for daylighting, researchers explored the benefits of full spectrum fluorescent lighting. Some of the pioneering research in the learning environment came from John Ott, who was known for his work in the cinematic use of time-lapse photography. Ott's experiments with different colored lighting systems and their effects on the health of plants, humans, and later on individual cells using time-lapsed micro-photography set the standard. In 1973, he examined the effect of full spectrum lighting using four first-grade classrooms in Sarasota, Florida (Ott, 1973, 1976). Using two windowless classrooms with full spectrum fluorescent lighting and two identical windowless classrooms with standard fluorescent fixtures, he observed and compared student activities in the four classrooms using time-lapsed concealed cameras. Photographs revealed that students under cool-white standard fluorescent lights exhibited decreased attention and greater hyperactivity, fatigue, and irritability than students under full spectrum lights. Full spectrum lights were able to calm handicapped students who exhibited extreme hyperactivity. This study also found one-third fewer dental cavities in students working under full spectrum fluorescent lights. Previous research studies conducted in 1930 with a large number of children showed that the incidence of dental cavities related to the amount of sunlight that children were exposed to; the higher the exposure, the fewer dental cavities. In all likelihood the effect can be attributed to the presence of vitamin D through skin photosynthesis.

Harry Wohlfarth conducted a five-year study in Canada and confirmed that full spectrum lights lower stress, decrease absenteeism, and improve overall achievement in the classroom (Wohlfarth and Sam, 1982; Wohlfarth, 1984; Wohlfarth and Gates, 1985). He observed that blood pressure dropped an average of 20 points per child and aggressive behavior decreased significantly under full spectrum lights. To further confirm the real effect of full spectrum light, the fixtures were changed back to standard fluorescent fixtures. After the change, behavior deteriorated.

In a study of 90 Swedish elementary school students, cortisol (a stress hormone) levels were measured and followed during the course of a year in four classrooms with varying daylighting levels. The results indicate that classrooms without daylight tend to disturb the basic hormone pattern and this in turn influences student concentration. Researchers concluded that this hormone disturbance could eventually have an impact on annual body growth and absenteeism (Kuller and Lindsten, 1992).

A number of recent studies in the United States claimed a relationship between daylighting and enhanced student performance and incited interest among education officials and advocates of daylighting. One major study analyzed the test scores of more than 21 000 students in three school districts in three states: California, Colorado, and Washington (Heschong Mahone Group, 1999b). This study included a particular focus on skylighting as a way to isolate illumination effects from other qualities associated with daylighting from windows, such as view and ventilation. Student performance data were obtained from three elementary school districts and statistical correlation analyses between performance and the amount of daylight were performed. The results of standardized tests were used as performance indicators and data from second to fifth grades were used. Students in classrooms with the most daylight progressed 20% on math tests and read 26% faster in reading tests. Classrooms with the most window area were associated with a 15–23% faster rate of improvement in math and reading. Classrooms with skylights were associated with 19–20% faster rate of

Figure 5.16   A typical classroom of the Durant Middle School in North Carolina designed by Innovative Design (courtesy of Innovative Design).

improvement and classrooms with operable windows were associated with 7–8% faster improvement.

Another study measured the benefits of daylighting in schools in the Johnston County and Wake County School Districts in North Carolina (Nicklas and Bailey, 1996). The study compared the scores of students from newly constructed daylit schools with those from schools that relied primarily on electric lighting. One of the newly constructed schools, the Durant Middle School, was designed with a top lighting system using roof monitors (Figure 5.16). According to the designer of this project, the building was laid out along an elongated east–west axis to take advantage of the southern orientation for natural daylighting and winter passive solar gain through the continuous single-sloped roof monitors. Overhangs and interior baffles shield any direct sunlight, providing better quality diffuse daylighting.

The academic performance of children in the new daylit classrooms was compared with student performance in other schools in the district that relied heavily on electric lighting. The results of the North Carolina study were similar to those found in the Heschong Mahone Group study. Students in the new daylit schools had higher reading and math achievement scores than students in buildings that relied heavily on electric lighting.

The results of these studies point to the positive effect of daylight in improving student learning. Whether this effect is due to chemical processes or physiological mechanisms remains to be investigated, but indications are clear that daylight influences learning in a very positive manner.

5.5 DAYLIGHT, WINDOWS AND THE THERAPEUTIC ENVIRONMENT

Sick people seem to improve faster when their hospital wards have windows with views of natural scenery, according to a study published in the journal *Science* (Ulrich, 1984). This study took place between 1972 and 1981 and examined the effect of windows and the quality of views on surgery patients in a suburban Pennsylvania hospital. Twenty-three patients assigned randomly to rooms with windows looking out on a natural scene had shorter post-operative hospital stays, received fewer negative comments in nurses' evaluations, and took fewer potent analgesics than 23 similar patients randomly assigned to rooms with windows facing a brick wall.

In windowless and underground spaces, people tend to suffer more fatigue and somatic distress, to express more negative feelings about the setting, and to show a clear preference for windowed places (Collins, 1975; Verderber, 1986; Heerwagen and Orians, 1986; Butler and Biner, 1989). Moreover, windows in hospital wards have been found to speed the recovery of hospital patients (Ulrich, 1984). The powerful effect of windows is felt not only among hospital patients who are confined to their rooms or beds but also among prison populations, where windows take on a meaning of life and freedom. Inmates with windows facing a meadow or mountains had significantly lower rates of stress-related sick calls than inmates with a view of the prison courtyard and buildings (Heerwagen and Heerwagen,1986). Inmates on the second floor had lower rates of stress-related sick calls because they benefited from the more expansive views from the second floor compared with the views experienced by inmates on the first floor.

The impact of daylighting on nonseasonal depression has been a subject of interest for medical researchers. Some have suggested that sunlight improves not only seasonal but also nonseasonal depression. Benedetti and colleagues (2001) examined the length of hospitalization in a sample of 415 unipolar and 187 bipolar depressed inpatients. Each of these groups was divided into two and patients were assigned either to rooms with eastern facing windows or to rooms with western exposures. The number of hospitalization days was used as a marker of the effect of sunlight. Bipolar patients receiving morning sunlight had a mean hospital stay 3.67 days shorter than that of patients whose rooms faced west and received afternoon sunlight. No effect was found in unipolar inpatients. Similarly, Beauchemin and Hays (1996) found a close relationship between sunny hospital rooms and the recovery period from severe refractory depression. In this study, half of the patients were placed in rooms that were bright and sunny and the other half were placed in rooms that lacked sunshine. Patients in sunny rooms had an average stay of 16.9 days compared with 19.5 days for patients in rooms that lacked sunshine.

Whether there are psychological or hormonal reactions that create the sensations of well-being that cause office workers to perform better, sick people to heal faster, or students in schools to do better scholastically, is an area of on-going research. Science has established the existence of a hormonal effect of light through the secretion of serotonin and cortisol during the day and melatonin at night. There are reasons to believe that a connection exists between psychological well-being and the hormonal reaction triggered by the lighting environment. Full spectrum lighting in the workplace significantly lowers stress levels, as has been shown in many studies. Ample evidence points towards the existence of hormonal and psychological processes, possibly a combination of both, that act on and invigorate our bodies through the action of daylight. Daylight is a source of health and well-being as vital as fresh air.

Daylighting strategies

6

Daylight has two components: sunlight, where the source is the sun, and skylight, where the source is the sky. Many but not all existing daylighting systems are designed to capture sunlight and admit it to the building. On a sunny day, as much as 100 000 lumen could be striking 1 m² of a building envelope, resulting in an illuminance of 100 000 lux. If the efficiency of the daylighting strategy were 100% that would be enough luminous energy to illuminate 100 m² at 1000 lux. The challenge in each daylighting strategy is to optimize the efficiency of the distribution system and, therefore, minimize the size of the collecting area. No daylighting system has 100% efficiency. Therefore, the size of the collecting area is linearly proportional to the efficiency of the system.

Daylighting strategies may be divided into two groups. The first includes sidelighting systems, where light is brought from the sides of a building into the interior space. A window is the simplest example of that strategy. The second group includes toplighting systems, where light is brought from the top of a building and distributed into the interior. A skylight is the simplest example of such a system.

A successful daylighting strategy is one that maximizes daylight levels inside the building but optimizes the quality of the luminous environment for the occupants. Daylighting design is not only about maximizing light levels. Excessive sunlight in an interior can be extremely uncomfortable for its occupants. The key word in daylighting design is control, not only of light levels but also of the direction and the distribution of light.

6.1   SIDELIGHTING SYSTEMS

Most sidelighting systems are designed to overcome the problem of uneven distribution of natural light resulting from the use of traditional side windows. Effective sidelighting systems operate by reducing excessive daylight levels near the windows and increasing them in areas away from the windows, thus giving rise to a more balanced daylight distribution throughout the room. Adding devices to the window glazing such as lightshelves, prisms or mirrored louvers offers a viable sidelighting strategy because of the ability of these devices to deflect light further away from the window wall and towards the back of the room.

Side window

Side windows include view and non-view elements, that is, windows and clerestory, respectively. Traditional side windows tend to produce overly lit areas near the window and dimmer conditions elsewhere, especially if the room is deep. The light distribution differs depending on sky conditions. Overcast skies provide a deeper penetration of diffuse daylight than clear skies; the shadows are, however, much softer and glare tends to be more severe because the sky is brighter (Robbins, 1986). In addition to sky conditions, factors that influence the spread and depth of daylight penetration include the orientation of the window, the location of the window within the wall and in relation to the rest of the room, the effective height of the window (from the sill to the upper limit of the window), and its width (Figure 6.1). Daylighting rules of thumb relate window head height to the depth of the daylit area adjacent to a façade and are expressed in design guidelines and norms in North America (O'Connor et al., 1997; Illuminating Engineering Society of North America (IESNA), 2000; United States Department of Energy (US-DOE), 2005), Canada (Enermodal Engineering Ltd for Public Works & Government Services Canada, 2002; Robertson, 2005; Reinhart, 2005), and in Europe (Cofaigh et al., 1999). An overall consensus suggests that the depth of the 'useful' daylit area ranges between 1.5 and 2.0 times the head height of the window (Figure 6.1). Besides the window head height, the width of the window also affects the depth of the useful daylit zone (Figures 6.2 and 6.3). A single side window may cause high discomfort glare because of the contrast between the brightness of the window and the darker background surrounding the window aperture. A more balanced daylight distribution may be obtained by bringing daylight from two different side walls, resulting in a deeper, more

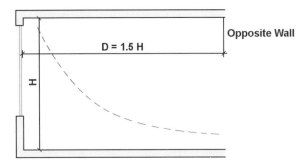

Figure 6.1 The effective depth (D) of daylight penetration from a side window as factor to window height (H).

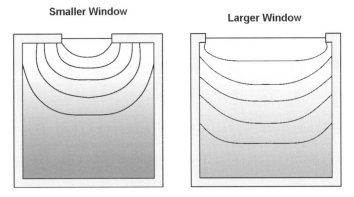

Figure 6.2 Isocontour curves of daylight penetration pattern under a narrow (a) and wide (b) side window.

balanced daylight distribution and a reduction in glare (Figures 6.3 and 6.4).

Clerestory system

A clerestory is also a side window but one that is placed high in the wall. It is usually contained in a part of the building that rises clear of the roof. Generally, it doesn't provide views towards the exterior but permits a deeper penetration of daylight into the room than a standard side window (Figure 6.5) while giving little glare discomfort to the occupants of the room. Like a standard side window, a south-facing clerestory will produce higher daylight illumination than one that faces north. East- and west-facing clerestories present the same problems as east and west windows: difficult shading and potentially high heat gains; however, sunlight penetration in the case of clerestories may not be as problematic as with standard side windows because the aperture is outside the field of view. The depth of the daylight zone depends on the

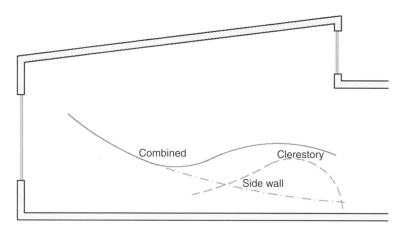

Figure 6.3 Balanced daylight penetration from two opposite side windows.

Figure 6.4 Daylight penetration from two adjacent side windows allows for more balanced daylight distribution and less glare.

mounting height of the clerestory (distance from the floor to the bottom of the aperture) and the width and length of the clerestory itself. The higher the mounting height, the deeper the daylight zone.

Combined side-systems

Combined side-systems that include a side window and a clerestory provide a more balanced distribution of daylight than does a typical side window or a clerestory window alone. Since daylight levels are additive, we can combine the daylight distribution from the side window with that from a clerestory window (Figures 6.6 and 6.7).

Lightshelf system

A lightshelf is a device designed to capture daylight, particularly sunlight, and redirect it towards the back of the room by

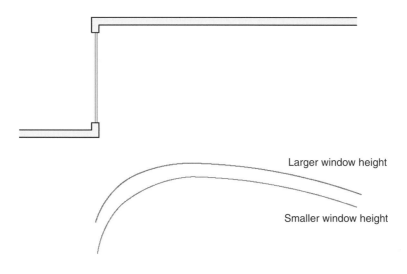

Larger window height

Smaller window height

Figure 6.5   Daylight penetration pattern with a clerestory window.

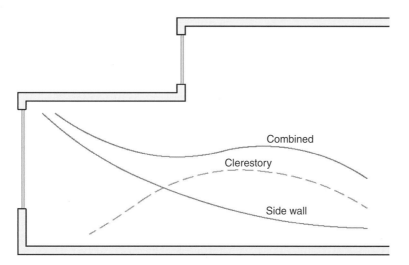

Combined

Clerestory

Side wall

Figure 6.6   Daylight penetration resulting from the combination of a vertical clerestory and a side window.

reflecting it off the ceiling. As a result, this strategy can lead to a more even distribution of light throughout the room than is found in a room with only a side window (Figure 6.8). A lightshelf divides the window into a lower part that mainly

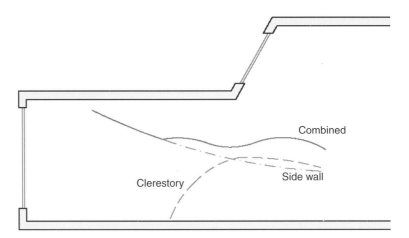

Figure 6.7 Daylight penetration resulting from the combination of an oblique clerestory and a side window.

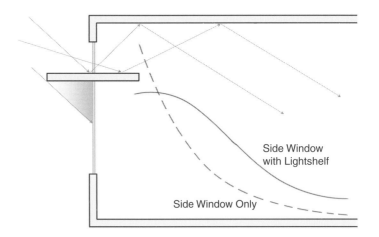

Figure 6.8 Daylight penetration from a combined lightshelf system.

serves the role of providing a view and an upper window that serves to redirect the daylight towards the back of the room away from the window plane. As a by-product, a light-shelf can also provide shade from direct sunlight and reduce glare from the sky. A lightshelf works best under sunlight conditions. The upper surface of the shelf is made of a highly reflective material to maximize reflection; it should not, however, be made of a specular (highly polished) surface, in order to prevent glare and shiny spots on the ceiling. Semi-specular surface materials are recommended.

The design of a lightshelf should be integrated with the fenestration of the building and planned during the early design stages. Its size and depth depend on window size and

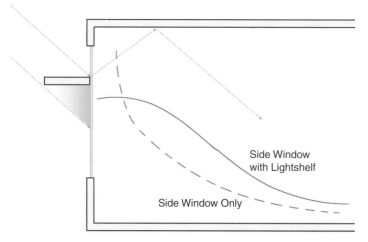

Figure 6.9 Daylight penetration in a room with an exterior lightshelf.

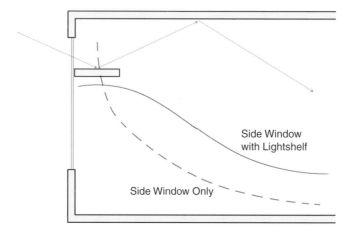

Figure 6.10 A comparison of daylight penetrations from a standard side window and one with an interior lightshelf.

façade orientation. A lightshelf may be combined (Figure 6.8), exterior only (Figure 6.9), or interior only (Figure 6.10). It can be horizontal or oblique (Figure 6.11). Exterior light-shelves are more effective in providing shade than interior ones but reflect less light towards the back of the room. Oblique lightshelves reflect light more deeply into the room but provide less shading than a horizontal lightshelf.

Variable area lightshelf system

A variation of the static lightshelf system, the variable area lightshelf is designed to be a dynamic system whereby the

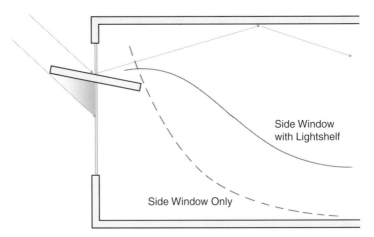

Side Window
with Lightshelf

Side Window Only

Figure 6.11   Daylight penetration in a room with an oblique lightshelf.

position of the lightshelf moves to optimize sunlight penetration according to time of day or season. As shown in Figure 6.12 (a) and (b) a highly reflective film moves between two positions to optimize reflection inside the space. This system can be automated for higher efficiency.

Louver systems

Like most effective sidelighting systems, louver systems are designed to capture sunlight falling in the front of the room and redirect it towards the back, thereby increasing daylight levels in the back of the room and reducing them in the front (Figure 6.13). Like the lightshelf and prism systems, the louver system works optimally under sunlight conditions. Louvers can be designed to be static or dynamic. In the latter case they are automatically controlled to follow the sun's movement in the sky. On a daily and seasonal basis, automated louvers tend to perform better than static ones but require calibration and algorithms that need adjustment depending on the illumination needs of the building as well as the heating and cooling requirements in order to admit the right amount of sunlight.

Prismatic systems

Prismatic glazing is designed to change the direction of incoming sunlight and redirect it by way of refraction and reflection. The basic operational principle of prismatic panels in sidelighting applications is depicted in Figures 6.14 and 6.15. As a ray of light hits the prism, its direction is altered because of refraction. A portion of it is then reflected upward towards the ceiling and onward towards the back of the room.

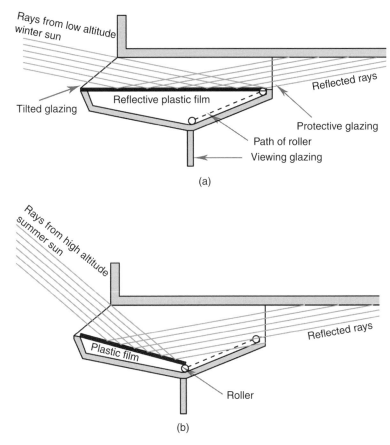

Figure 6.12 The variable area lightshelf system with two positions, one favoring low sun angles (a) and the other high sun angles (b).

The use of prismatic glass is not a novelty but has been frequently utilized in electric lighting applications, mainly to scatter and distribute light more optimally. However, its application as a daylighting system to harvest and control light distribution in building interiors has been limited and its performance as a viable daylighting solution remains to be researched and further explored. In principle, the prismatic panel can be placed in the upper portion of a side window to deflect a portion of the incoming light deeper into the room. In the case of double or triple glazing, the prismatic panel can be sandwiched between glass panels to minimize dust and maintenance.

Anidolic zenithal collector system

The zenithal anidolic system is comprised of two concentrating mirrors of parabolic shape that capture the incoming

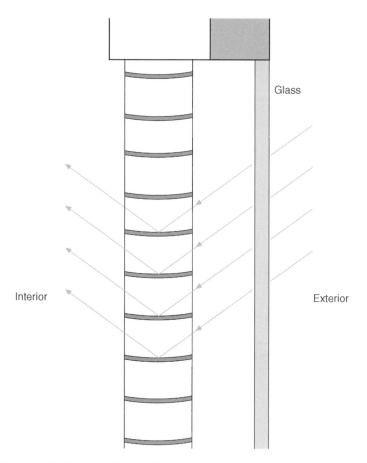

Figure 6.13   Light-redirecting louver system.

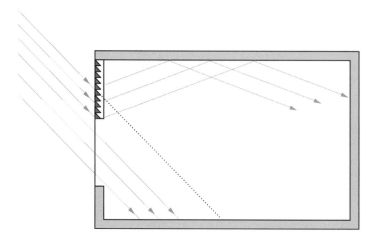

Figure 6.14   Prismatic panel inserted within a side window redirecting incoming sunlight.

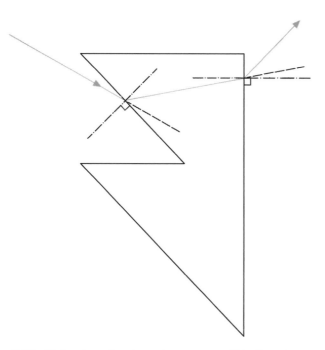

Figure 6.15   Refraction of an incoming sun ray within the prism provoking a change of direction and improving sunlight penetration towards the back of room.

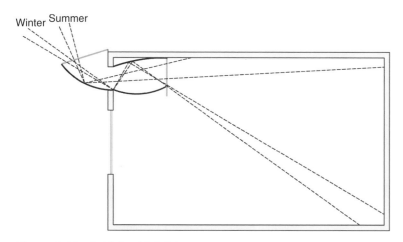

Figure 6.16   Anidolic sidelighting system.

light flux over a wider area and distribute it inside a room (Figure 6.16). It is designed to increase light levels deep into the room and create a more balanced daylight distribution throughout the space. The anidolic system can be coupled with a light duct to channel light by inter-reflection within the light tube and distribute it inside a room in a more control-led manner.

6.2 TOPLIGHTING SYSTEMS

Skylight system

A skylight system is one of the simplest toplighting strategies. It usually provides a horizontal or slanted opening in the roof of a building and is designed to capture sunlight when the sun is high in the sky and diffuse light from the zenithal area of the sky vault, and introduce it into the portion of the room under the skylight. This daylighting approach can be used only for the top floor of a multi-story building or for single-story buildings. Several skylights uniformly distributed across the ceiling lead to a uniform distribution of daylight. A skylight gives daylight distribution of an inverted V-shape (Figure 6.17), where daylight is maximum underneath the skylight and progressively lessens as we move away from that area. The reflector shown in Figure 6.18 is used to deflect light from the area beneath the skylight in order to obtain a more even distribution of light throughout the room. When several skylights are used, and under diffuse sky conditions, the recommended spacing between them is equal to their mounting height in order to obtain a fairly uniform distribution of daylight throughout the space (Figure 6.19).

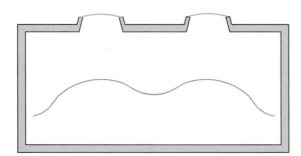

Figure 6.17   Daylight penetration pattern from two skylights.

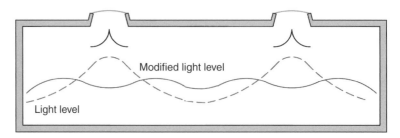

Figure 6.18   Modified daylight penetration pattern with a light deflecting device beneath the skylight.

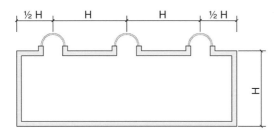

Figure 6.19   Rule of thumb for spacing skylights to obtain uniform light distribution beneath multiple skylights.

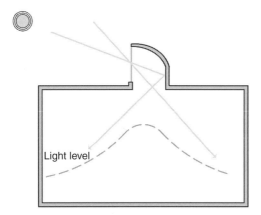

Figure 6.20   A single-sided roof monitor system designed to allow winter sunlight to enter but not summer sunlight.

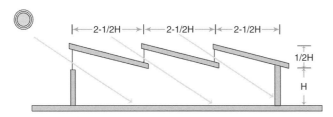

Figure 6.21   A single-sided sawtooth system provides directional distribution of daylight inside the room.

Roof monitor and sawtooth systems

Roof monitors (Figure 6.20) and sawtooth systems (Figure 6.21) are toplighting strategies that differ primarily in their shapes. Under these systems, light is captured through vertical or sloped openings in the roof. These openings can be designed to capture sunlight at certain times of the day or of the year, depending on the requirements of the building. Roof monitors can be single-sided or two-sided. Single-sided

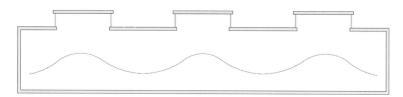

Figure 6.22 Two-sided roof monitor system.

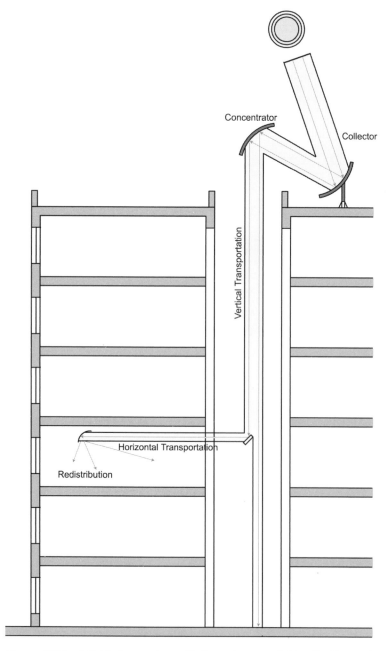

Figure 6.23 A light pipe system with its various sunlight collection and light transport systems.

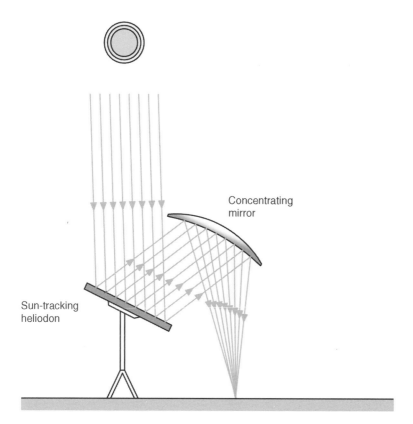

Concentrating
mirror

Sun-tracking
heliodon

Figure 6.24   A sun-tracking heliodon with a concentrating mirror.

roof monitors and sawtooth systems provide a directional effect inside the room, especially if the elements are spaced far apart. Two-sided roof monitors provide a more uniform distribution of daylight and less directionality, particularly under overcast sky conditions (Figure 6.22).

Light pipe system

A light pipe system is a toplighting strategy designed to bring daylight into the lower floors of a multi-story building. This apparatus can be relatively simple or sophisticated and elaborate. The typical components of a light pipe system are a solar collector that gathers sunlight, a concentrator that focuses solar energy onto a smaller area, a transport system, and a distribution system (Figure 6.23). The solar collector may be a simple stationary mirror or a sophisticated computerized heliodon that tracks the sun's movement (Figure 6.24). Another possible component of a light pipe system is a solar concentrator that is made of a concentrating mirror or lens that focuses the energy collected from a large collector

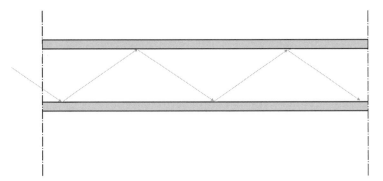

Figure 6.25   The light transport principle by way of inter-reflection within the walls of a fiber optic.

onto a smaller area so that it can be transported efficiently. The higher the concentration ratio of the mirror or the lens, the smaller the cross-section of the transporting mechanism needs to be. The transport system can be a simple opening shaft through the various floors of a building as shown in Figure 6.23, or it can be a prism or fiber optic system that channels light in whatever direction is needed. Light is transported within the fiber optic walls by being inter-reflected within the walls of the fiber (Figure 6.25).

Conclusion

7

When properly designed, daylighting can provide significant energy savings for building owners. With recent concerns over global warming and the need to conserve fossil fuels, it is imperative to use daylighting as a primary strategy for building illumination.

Daylight, or the lack thereof, affects in no small way the psychological and physiological health of building occupants and their overall well-being. In addition, windows connect those who are confined indoors with the outdoors and allow them to feel closer to nature. The lack of sunlight can even prove toxic because it leads to a deficiency of vitamin D in our bodies. Buildings should be designed to maximize our exposure to sunlight in order to facilitate the cutaneous photosynthesis that supplies most or all of our vitamin D needs.

Vitamin D is vital to our lives and is the first defense against such ailments as cancer, osteoporosis, diabetes, multiple sclerosis, and other immune system diseases. We need only 15 to 35 minutes a day of outdoor exposure to sunlight three or four times per week to generate an adequate amount of vitamin D, which is estimated to be between 120 and 150 nanomoles per litre of blood. Many of us, however, do not receive adequate exposure to sunlight because of climate, working conditions, health problems, or age. Some of us are bedridden or old and not very mobile, thereby limiting our exposure to sunlight. Because glass filters out about 95% of the UV-B radiation, the length of exposure to sunlight indoors must be nine or ten times longer than the recommended outdoor exposure. Buildings that house the elderly have even higher requirements for sunlight because aged skin diminishes the cutaneous photosynthesis of vitamin D.

Many of us spend most of the daytime hours at work and may be unable to come into contact with daylight outside our work schedules. As a result, buildings should be designed to admit light levels that will enable us to maintain a well-balanced circadian rhythm. High daylight levels optimize the secretion of serotonin and keep us alert. In addition to vitamin D, a well-balanced circadian rhythm that includes adequate amounts of serotonin during the day and melatonin at night appears to boost our immune systems and allows our natural defense mechanisms to fend off many ailments including cancer, diabetes, and multiple sclerosis. Because we spend the majority of our lifetime indoors, buildings should be considered as healing places in addition to their traditional role as shelter. Buildings that don't admit sunlight provoke disease, either directly or indirectly.

Daylight is one of the most effective antidepressants available. Research has shown that light levels above 2500 lux can offset Seasonal Affective Disorder (SAD); however, illuminance levels of 10 000 lux have been shown to be four times more efficient. These illuminance levels are significantly higher than those generally recommended for most visual tasks. Needless to say, we cannot rely on electric lighting systems to supply such high illuminance levels. Daylighting, however, can supply such levels and, as result, helps to alleviate 80% of SAD disorders. The spectral quality of light also plays a significant role in the fight against SAD and nonseasonal depression, and in the production of vitamin D through the skin. High illuminance combined with the full spectrum quality of daylight make daylighting the most economical and perhaps the only plausible solution. Designers may not be able to meet this need for exposure to sunlight everywhere in a building. They can, however, incorporate solariums, balconies, atria, and terraces where building occupants can have access to unfiltered sunlight.

References

Aarts, M. (1994). Towards a new kind of office lighting: study for a human interactive lighting system. Unpublished Master's thesis, Technical University of Eindhoven, The Netherlands.

Acheson, E., Bachrach, C.A. and Wright, F.M. (1960). Some comments on the relationship of the distribution of multiple sclerosis to latitude, solar radiation and other variables. *Acta Pshychiatrica Scandinavica* 35(suppl. 147), 132–47.

Alimoglu, M.K. and Donmez, L. (2005). Daylight exposure and the other predictors of burnout among nurses in a university hospital. *International Journal of Nursing Studies* 42, 549–55.

American Cancer Society (2007). *Cancer Facts and Figures 2007*. Atlanta, GA: American Cancer Society. Also available online at http://www.cancer.org/downloads/STT/2008CAFFfinalsecured.pdf. Last accessed 18 January 2007.

Archer, J.W. (1998). Daylighting and Canadian building codes. In: *Proceedings of the Daylighting '98 Conference*. International Conference on Daylighting Technologies for Energy Efficiency in Building, 11–13 May, Ottawa, Ont., 287–88.

Audy, J.R. and Duan, F.L. (1974). Community health. In: Sargent, F., ed., *Human Ecology*. Amsterdam: North Holland, pp. 345–63.

Australia DCP (2002). [Online] Available from: http://www.cityofsydney.nsw.gov.au/council/documents/OnExhibition/ESDRatingTool/IEQ-4%20Daylight.pdf [Accessed June 2008].

Avery, D.H., Eder, D.N., Bolte, M.A., Hellekson, C.J., Dunner, D.L., Vitiello, M.V. and Prinz, P.N. (2001). Dawn simulation and bright light in the treatment of SAD: a controlled study. *Biological Psychiatry* 50(3), 205–16.

Baker, P. (1998). *Prescriptions for a Healthy House: A Practical Guide for Architects, Builders and Homeowners*. Santa Fe: Inword Press.

Barnaby, J.F. (1980). Lighting for productivity gains. *Lighting Design + Application* 10(2), 20–28.

Baron, R.A., Rea, M.S. and Daniels, S.G. (1992). Effects of indoor lighting (illuminance and spectral distribution) on the performance of cognitive tasks and interpersonal behaviors: the potential mediating role of positive affect. *Motivation and Emotion* 16, 1–33.

Beauchemin, K.M. and Hays, P. (1996). Sunny hospital rooms expedite recovery from severe and refractory depressions. *Journal of Affective Disorders* 40(1–2), 49–51.

Belcher, C.M. and Kluczny, R. (1987). Lighting ergonomics and the decision process. *Proceedings of the 8th Annual Meeting of the ASEM*, 51–55.

Benedetti, F., Colombo, C., Barbini, B., et al. (2001). Morning sunlight reduces length of hospitalization in bipolar depression. *Journal of Affective Disorders* 62(3), 221–23.

Blackwell, H.R. (1959). The development and use of a quantitative method for specifications of interior illumination levels on the basis of perform-ance data. *Illum Eng* 54, 317–53.

Blask, D.E., Sauer, L.A., Dauchy, R.T., et al. (1999). New insights into mela-tonin regulation of cancer growth. *Advances in Experimental Medecine and Biology* 460, 337–43.

Blask, D.E., Dauchy, R.T. and Sauer, L.A. (2005). Putting cancer to sleep at night: the neuroendocrine/circadian melatonin signal. *Endocrine* 27, 179–88.

Borimir, J. and Perlin, J. (1979). Solar energy use and litigation in ancient times. *Solar Law Reporter* 1(3), 583–94.

Borisova, A. (2003). The effect of vitamin D3 on insulin secretion and periph-eral insulin sensitivity in type 2 diabetic patients. *International Journal of Clinical Practice* 57(4), 258–61.

Boubekri, M. (2004a). Daylighting design standards. *Journal of the Human–Environment System* 7(2), 57–64.

Boubekri, M. (2004b). An argument for daylighting legislation because of health. *Journal of the Human–Environment System* 7(2), 57–64.

Boubekri, M. and Boyer, L.L. (1992). Effect of window size and sunlight pres-ence on glare. *Lighting Research and Technology* 24(2), 69–74.

Boubekri, M. and Haghighat, F. (1993). Windows and environmental sat-isfaction: a survey study of an office building. *Indoor Environment* 3(2), 164–72.

Boubekri, M., Hull, B.R. and Boyer, L.L. (1991). Effect of sunlight penetra-tion on office occupants' mood and satisfaction: a novel way of assessing sunlight. *Environment & Behavior* 23(4), 474–93.

Boyce, P.R. (1973). Age, illumination, visual performance, and preference. *Lighting Research and Technology* 5, 125–44.

British Standards Institute (1982). *BS8206 Part 2: Code of Practice for Daylighting*. BSI.

Brown, A., Dusso, A. and Slatopolsky, E. (1999). Vitamin D. *American Journal of Physiology* 277(2 Pt 2), F1757–75.

Brown, G.H., Young, S.N., Gruthler, S., et al. (1979). Melatonin in human cerebrospinal fluid in daytime: its origin and variation with age. *Life Sciences* 25, 929–36.

Browning, W. (1992). NMB Bank Headquarters. Urban Land Institute, *Urban Land*, June (summer volume).

Building Officials & Code Administrators (1990). *The BOCA National Building Code/1990*. BOCA International Inc., pp. 126–27.

Bunker, J.W.M. and Harris, R.S. (1937). Precise evaluation of ultraviolet therapy in experimental rickets. *New England Journal of Medecine* 216, 165–69.

Butler, D.L. and Biner, P.M. (1989). Effects of setting on window preferences and factors associated with those preferences. *Environment and Behavior* 21, 17–31.

Butti, K. and Perlin, J.A. (1980). *Golden Thread: 2500 Years of Solar Architecture and Technology*. Palo Alto: Cheshire Books; New York: Van Nostrand Reinhold.

Campbell, S.S., Kriptke, D.F., Gillin, J.C., et al. (1988). Exposure to light in healthy elderly subjects and Alzheimer' patients. *Physiology and Behaviour* 42, 141–44.

Cancer Council Australia (2005). Osteoporosis Australia and other health organ-isations. Available from: www.cancer.org.au/policy/positionstatements/sunsmart/risksandbenefitsofsunexposure.htm (cited June 2007).

Cassel, J. (1976). The contribution of the social environment to host resistance. *American Journal of Epidemiology* 104, 107–23.

Chadwick, E. (1842). *Report on the Sanitary Condition of the Labouring Population of Great Britain*. Flinn, M.W., ed., Edinburgh: Edinburgh University Press.

Chauvel, P. and Dogniaux, R. (1982). Glare from windows: current views of the problem. *Lighting Research and Technology* 14, 31–46.

Chen, S., Ni, X.P., Humphreys, M.H., et al. (2005). 1,25 dihydroxyvitamin D amplifies type A natriuretic peptide receptor expression and activity in target cells. *Journal of the American Society of Nephrology* 16, 329–39.

Chen, T.C. and Holick, M.F. (2003). Vitamin D and prostate cancer prevention and treatment. *Trends in Endocrinology and Metabolism* 14, 423–30.

Chui, K. (2004). Hypovitaminosis D is associated with insulin resistance and betta cell dysfunction. *American Journal of Clinical Nutrition* 79, 820–25.

Cofaigh, E.O., Fitzgerald, E., Alcock, R., et al. (1999). *A Green Vitruvius – Principles and Practice of Sustainable Architectural Design*. London: James & James.

Cohen, M., Lippman, M. and Chabner, B. (1978). Role of pineal gland in the aetiology and treatment of breast cancer. *Lancet* 2, 814–16.

Cohen, M.J. (1984). *Culture-Nature-Self Paradigm*. Athens GA: Journal of Instructional Psychology, Summer volume, Athens, Georgia.

Colas, C., Garabedian, M., Fontbonne, A., et al. (1988). Insulin secretion and plasma 1,25(OH)2D after UV-B irradiation in healthy adults. *Hormone and Metabolic Research* 21, 154–55.

Collins, B.L. (1975). *Windows and People: A Literature Survey: Psychological Reaction to Environments with and without Windows*. National Bureau of Standards Building Science Series 70, U.S. Department of Commerce.

Davenport, C., et al. (1922). Multiple Sclerosis from the standpoint of geographic distribution and race. *Archives of Neurology and Psychiatry* 8, 51–58.

DeLuca, H.F. (1988). The vitamin D story: a collaborative effort of basic science and clinical medicine. *The FASEB Journal* 2, 224–36.

DeMarini, D.M., Abu-Shakra, A., Felton, C.F., et al. (1995). Mutation spectra in salmonella of chlorinated, chloraminated, or ozonated drinking water extracts: comparison to MX. *Environmental and Molecular Mutagenesis* 26(4), 270–85.

Department of the Environment (1971). *Sunlight and Daylight Planning Criteria and Design of Buildings*. London: HSMO. pp. 22–26.

Dubos, R. (1965). *Man Adapting*. New Haven: Yale University Press.

Eastman, C.I., Young, M.A., Fogg, L.F., et al. (1998). Bright light treatment of winter depression. *Archives of General Psychiatry* 55, 883–89.

El-Sonbaty, M.R. and Abdul-Ghaffar, N.U.A.M.A. (1996). Vitamin D deficiency in veiled Kuwaiti women. *European Journal of Clinical Nutrition* 32, 338–39.

Energy Information Administration (1998). *Annual Energy Outlook, with Projections to 2015*. Washington DC: U.S. Department of Energy.

Enermodal Engineering Ltd for Public Works & Government Services Canada. (2002). *Daylighting Guide for Canadian Commercial Buildings*.

Erikson, C. and Kuller, R. (1983). Non-visual effects of office lighting. *Proceedings of the 20th Session of the Commission Internationale de l'Eclairage*, pp. D602/1–4, Amsterdam, June 23–25, Commission Internationale de l'Eclairage.

Erkal, M.Z., Wilde, J., Bilgin, Y., et al. (2006). High prevalence of vitamin D deficiency, secondary hyperparathyroidism and generalized bone pain in Turkish immigrants in Germany: identification of risk factors. *Osteoporosis International* 17, 1133–40.

Espiritu, R.C., Kripke, D.F., Ancoli-Israel, S., et al. (1994). Low illumination experienced by San Diego adults: association with atypical depressive symptoms. *Biological Psychiatry* 35, 403–407.

Finer, S.E. (1952). *The Life and Times of Sir Edwin Chadwick*. London: Methuen.

Fisher, G. (1995). The birth of the prison retold. *The Yale Law Journal* 104(6), 1235–324.

Flynn, J.E. (1977). A study of subjective responses to low energy and nonuniform lighting systems. *Lighting Design and Application* 7(2), 6–15.

Forman, A.D., Stoller, J.K. and Horsburgh, C.R. (1996). Healing by design. *New England Journal of Medecine* 334, 334–36.

Fuller, K. (2003). Sad to the bone. *Nursing Homes Long Term Care Management* 44–51.

Gannage-Yared, M.H., Chemali, R., Yaacoub, N., et al. (2000). Hypovitaminosis D in a sunny country: relation to lifestyle and bone markers. *Journal of Bone and Mineral Research* 15, 1856–62.

Garland, C. and Garland, F. (1980). Do sunlight and vitamin D reduce the likelihood of colon cancer? *International Journal of Epidemiology* 9, 227–31.

Garland, C., Comstock, G., Garland, F., et al. (1989). Serum 25–hydroxyvitamin D and colon cancer: eight–year prospective study. *The Lancet* 2, 1176–78.

Ghannam, N.N., Hammami, M.M., Bakheet, S.M., et al. (1999). Bone mineral density of the spine and femur in healthy Saudi females: relation to vitamin D status, pregnancy, and lactation. *Calcified Tissue International* 65, 23–28.

Gibson, J.J. (1971). The information available in pictures. *Leonardo Journal* 4, 27. Great Britain: Pergamon Press.

Gillie, O. (2006). A new government policy is needed for sunlight and vitamin D. *British Journal of Dermatology* 154(6), 1052–61.

Giovannucci, E. (1998). Dietary influences of 1,25(OH)2 vitamin D in relation to prostate cancer: a hypothesis. *Cancer Causes Control* 9, 567–82.

Glerup, H., Mikkelsen, K., Poulsen, L., et al. (2000). Commonly recommended daily intake of vitamin D is not sufficient if sunlight exposure is limited. *Journal of Internal Medicine* 247, 260–68.

Glisson, F. (1650). *De Rachitide sive morbo puerili, qui vulgo The Rickets diciteur*. London: G. Du-gardi, 1–416.

Glorieux, F.H. and Feldman, D. (eds) (1997). *Vitamin D*. San Diego CA: Academic Press.

Goldblatt, H. and Soames, K.N. (1923). A study of rats on a normal diet irradiated daily by the mercury vapor quartz lamp or kept in darkness. *Biochemical Journal* 17, 294–97.

Gordon, S. (2007). Urban women may have greater breast cancer risk. www.MedicineNet.com, document viewed December 2003.

Gorham, E.D., Garland, C.F., Garland, F.C., et al. (2005). Holick, Vitamin D and prevention of colorectal cancer. *Journal of Steroid Biochemistry and Molecular Biology* 97, 179–94.

Graham, J.W. (1972). Notes on houses and housing-districts at Abdera and Himera. *American Journal of Archaeology* 76(3), 295–301.

Grant, M. (author and translator) and Oribasius (1997). *Dieting for an Emperor: A Translation of Books 1 and 4 of Oribasius' "Medical Compilations"*. Leiden: Brill Academic Publishers.

Grant, W. (2004). *Vitamin D: requirements for optimal health*. Presented to Smart Life Forum, Palo Alto CA, 21 October 2004.

Grant, W.B. and Garland, C.F. (2006). The association of solar ultraviolet B (UVB) with reducing risk of cancer: multifactorial ecologic analysis of geographic variation in age–adjusted cancer mortality rates. *Anticancer Research* 26, 2687–700.

Graw, P., Haug, H-J., Leonhardt, G., et al. (1998). Sleep deprivation response in seasonal affective disorder during a 40-h constant routine. *Journal of Affective Disorders* 48(1), 69–74.

Graw, P., Recker, S., Sand, L., et al. (1999). Winter and summer outdoor light exposure in women with and without seasonal affective disorder. *Journal of Affective Disorders* 56, 163–69.

Grivas, T.B. and Savvidou, O.D. (2007). Melatonin the 'light of night' in human biology and adolescent idiopathic scoliosis. *Scoliosis* 4 April, 2:6.

Hartkopf, V., Loftness, V., Duckworth, S., et al. (1994). *The Intelligent Workplace Retrofit Initiative: DOE Building Studies*. Produced under contract for the U.S. Department of Energy, December 1994.

Health & Safety Commission (1992). *Workplace (Health Safety and Welfare) Regulations 1992: Approved Code of Practice and Guidance L24*. London: HMSO.

Heerwagen, J.H. and Heerwagen, D.R. (1986). Lighting and psychological comfort. *Lighting Design & Application* 16, 47–51.

Heerwagen, J.H. and Orians, G.H. (1986). Adaptation to windowlessness: a study of the visual decor in windowed and windowless offices. *Environment and Behavior* 18, 623–39.

Heerwagen, J.H., Heubach, J.G., Montgomery, J., et al. (1995). Environmental design, work, and well-being: managing occupational stress through changes in the workplace environment. *AAOHN Journal: Official journal of the American Association of Occupational Health Nurses* 43(9), 458–68.

Heisler, G. (2005). Health impacts of ultraviolet radiation in urban ecosystems: a review. In: *Proceedings of SPIE Vol. 5886 Ultraviolet Ground- and Space-based Measurements, 1 Models, and Effects V*. Bellingham WA: SPIE.

Heschong Mahone Group (1999a). *Skylighting and Retail Sales*. 20 August 1999. Available from: www.h-m-g.com/projects/daylighting/summaries%20on%20daylighting.htm#Skylighting_and_Retail_Sales%20-%20PG&E%201999

Heschong Mahone Group (1999b). *Daylighting in Schools*. Pacific Gas and Electric Company on behalf of the California Board for Energy Efficiency Third Party Program.

Hesselgren, S. (1975). *Man's Perception of Man-made Environment*. Lund: Studentlitteratur ab.

Holick, M.F. (1999). Vitamin D. In: Shils, M.E., eds, *Modern Nutrition in Health and Disease*. Baltimore MD: Williams and Wilkins, pp. 329–45.

Holick, M.F. (2004). Sunlight and vitamin D in the prevention of cancers, type 1 diabetes, heart disease, and osteoporosis. *American Journal of Clinical Nutrition* 79, 362–71.

Holick, M.F. (2006). Vitamin D: Its role in cancer prevention and treatment. *Progress in Biophysics & Molecular Biology* 92, 49–59.

Holick, M.F., Matsuoka, L.Y. and Wortsman, J. (1989). Age, vitamin D, and solar ultraviolet. *The Lancet* 2, 1104–105.

Hollwich, F. (1979). *The Influence of Ocular Light Perception on etabolism in Man and in Animal*. New York: Springer Verlag.

Hopkinson, R.G. (1965). The psychophysics of sunlighting. *Sunlighting in Buildings: Proceedings of the CIE Intersessional Conference, University of Newcastle-upon-Tyne, 5–9 April*. pp. 13–26.

Hopkinson, R.G., Petherbridge, P. and Longmore, J. (1966). *Daylighting*. London: Heinemann.

Horowitz, T., Cade, B., Wolfe, J., et al. (2001). Efficacy of bright light and sleep/darkness scheduling in alleviating circadian maladaptation to night work. *American Journal of Physiology–Endocrinology and Metabolism* 281, 384–91.

Howard, E. (1902). *Garden Cities of To-Morrow*. London, 1902. Reprinted, edited with a Preface by F.J. Osborn and an Introductory Essay by Lewis Mumford. London: Faber and Faber, [1946], pp. 50–57, 138–47.

Hrushesky, W.J. (1985). Circadian timing of cancer chemotherapy. *Science* 228, 73–75.

Hrushesky, W.J. (2001). Tumor chronobiology. *Journal of Controlled Release* 74, 27–30.

Hughes, P.C. and McNelis, J.F. (1978). Lighting, productivity, and the work environment. *Lighting Design + Application* 8(12), 32–39.

Illuminating Engineering Society of North America (2000). *The Lighting Handbook*, Distributed through the IESNA, 9th edition, New York.

Inderjeeth, C.A., Barrett, T., Al-Lahham, Y., et al. (2002). Seasonal variation, hip fracture and vitamin D levels in Southern Tasmania. *New Zealand Medical Journal* 26(1152), 183–85.

Inouye, S.T. and Kawamura, H. (1979). Persistence of circadian rhythmicity in a mammalian hypothalamic 'Island' containing the suprachiasmatic nucleus. *Proceedings of the National Academy of Science USA* 76(11), 5962–66.

Iqbal, S.J., Kaddam, I., Wassif, W., et al. (1994). Continuing clinically severe vitamin D deficiency in Asians in the UK (Leicester). *Postgraduate Medical Journal* 70, 708–14.

Isen, A.M., Means, B., Patrick, R., et al. (1982). Some factors influencing decision-making strategy and risk taking. In Clark, M. and Fiske, S., eds, *Affect and Cognition*. Hillsdale NJ: Lawrence Erlbaum Associates, Inc., pp. 243–61.

Ishii, C., Suzuki, H., Baba, T., et al. (2001). Seasonal variation of glycemic control in type 2 diabetic patients. *Diabetes Care* 24, 1503.

John, E.M., Schwartz, G.G., Dreon, D.M., et al. (1999). Vitamin D and breast cancer risk: the NHANES/Epidemiologic follow-up study, 1971–1975 to 1992. National Health and Nutrition Examination Survey. *Cancer Epidemiology Biomarkers & Prevention* 8, 399–406.

Julian, W. (1998). Daylighting standards, codes and policies. In: *Proceedings of the Daylighting '98 Conference. International Conference on Daylighting Technologies for Energy Efficiency in Building, May 11–13, Ottawa (Canada)*. 265–69.

Knowles, R. (1979). Right to light. *Progressive Architecture* 76–81.

Knowles, R. (1980). Solar access and urban form. *AIA Journal* 69(2), 42–49.

Knudsen, A. and Benford, F. (1938). Quantitative studies of the effectiveness of ultraviolet radiation of different wavelengths on rickets. *Journal of Biological Chemistry* 124, 287–99.

Koga, Y. and Nakamura, H. (1998). Daylighting codes, standards and policies mainly in Japan, In: *Proceedings of the Daylighting '98 Conference. International Conference on Daylighting Technologies for Energy Efficiency in Building, May 11–13, Ottawa (Canada)*. pp. 279–86.

Krause, R., Buhring, M., Hopfenmuller, W., et al. (1998). Ultraviolet B and blood pressure. *The Lancet* 352, 709–10.

Kreiter, S.R., Schwartz, R.P., Kirkman, H.N., Jr., et al. (2000). Nutritional rickets in African American breast-fed infants. *Journal of Pediatrics* 137, 153–57.

Kriptke, D.F., Mullaney, D.J., Savides, T.J., et al. (1989). Phototherapy for non-seasonal major depressive disorders. In Rosenthal, N.E. and Blehar, N.C., eds, *Seasonal Affective Disorders and Phototherapy*. New York: The Guilford Press, pp. 342–56.

Kuller, R. and Lindsten, C. (1992). Health and behavior of children in classrooms with and without windows. *Journal of Environmental Psychology* 12, 305–17.

Kwartler, M. and Masters, R. (1984). Daylight as a zoning device for Midtown. *Energy & Buildings* 6, 175–89.

Lam, R.W., Tam, E.M., Yathan, L.N., et al. (2001). Seasonal depression: the dual vulnerability hypothesis revisited. *Journal of Affective Disorders* 63(1–3), 123–32.

Landin-Wilhelmsen, K., Wilhelmsen, L., Wilske, J., et al. (1995). Sunlight increases serum 25(OH)vitamin D concentration whereas 1,25(OH) 2D3 is unaffected. Results from a general population study in Goteborg, Sweden (The WHO MONICA Project). *European Journal of Clinical Nutrition* 49(6), 400–407.

Leproult, R., Colecchia, E.F., L'Hermite-Bale'riaux, M., et al. (2001). Transitions from dim to bright light in the morning induces an immediate elevation of cortisol levels. *Journal of Clinical Endocrinology and Metabolism* 86, 151–57.

Leslie, R.P. and Hartleb, S.B. (1990). Human response and variability in the luminous environment. In: *Proceedings of the CIBSE National Lighting Conference, 8–11 April 1990, Cambridge, England*. London: Chartered Institute of Building Services Engineers, pp. 87–99.

Lindheim, R. (1983). Environment, people and health. *Annual Review of Public Health* 4, 335–59.

Littlefair, P. (1999). *Daylighting and Solar Control in Building Regulations*. Building Research Establishment. CR398/99, pp. 1–27.

MacLaughlin, J. and Holick, M.F. (1985). Ageing decreases the capacity of human skin to produce vitamin D. 3. *Journal of Clincal Investigation* 76, 1536–38.

Markus, T.A. (1967). The function of windows – a reappraisal. *Building Science* 2, 97–121.

Maslach, C. and Jackson, S. (1996). *Maslach Burnout Inventory*. Palo Alto CA: Psychologist's Press.

Mawer, E.B., Backhouse, J., Holman, C.A., et al. (1972). The distribution and storage of vitamin D and its metabolites in human tissues. *Clinical Science* 43, 413–31.

Mayo, E. (1933). *The Human Problems of an Industrial Civilization*. Boston: Harvard University Press, Graduate School of Business Administration.

McColl, S. and Veitch, J. (2001). *Full-spectrum Fluorescent Lighting: A Review of its Effects on Physiology and Health*. Cambridge University Press.

Mehrabian, A. and Russell, J.A. (1974). *An Approach to Environmental Psychology*. Cambridge: MIT Press.

Miller, S.S. (1976). Let the sunshine in: a comparison of Japanese and American solar rights. *Harvard Environmental Law* 1, 579.

Ministère d'Education (1977). *Cahier des recommendations techniques de construction* Editions du Service de l'Education National, France.

Moore, R.Y. and Eichler, V.B. (1972). Loss of a circadian adrenal corticosterone rhythm following suprachiasmatic lesions in the rat. *Brain Research* 42, 201–206.

Morgan, M.H. (1914). *Vitruvius: the Ten Books on Architecture*. Cambridge: Harvard University Press; London: Humphrey Milford, Oxford University Press, p. 3.

Multiple Sclerosis Society Statistics (2006). Available from www.nationalmssociety.org, last accessed 16 March 2006.

Nasca, P.C., Burnett, W.S., Greenwald, P., et al. (1980). Population density as an indicator of urban–rural differences in cancer incidence, upstate New York, 1968–1972. *American Journal of Epidemiology* 112(3), 362–75.

National Sleep Foundation (2005). The 2005 NSF National Sleep in America Poll. Available: http://www.sleepfoundation.org. [accessed 15 January 2007].

Nayyar, K. and Cochrane, R. (1996). Seasonal changes in affective state measured prospectively and retrospectively. *British Journal of Psychiatry* 168(5), 627–32.

Ne'eman, E. and Hopkinson, R.G. (1970). Critical minimum acceptable window size: a study of window design and provision of a view. *Lighting Research and Technology* 2, 17–27.

Ne'eman, E. and Longmore, J. (1973). Physical aspects of windows: integration of daylight with artificial light. *Proceedings of CIE Conference Istanbul, on Windows and their Function in Architectural Design*. Istanbul. Vienna, Austria: Commission Internationale de l'Eclairage.

Ne'eman, E., Sweitzer, G. and Vine, E. (1984). Office worker response to lighting and daylighting issues in workspace environments: a pilot survey. *Energy and Buildings* 6, 159–71.

Neer, R., Clark, M., Friedman, V., et al. (1977). Environmental and nutritional influences on plasma 25-hydroxyvitamin D concentration and calcium metabolism in man. In: Norman, A.W., Schaefer, K., Coburn, J.W., DeLuca, H.F., Fraser, D., Grigoleit, H.G. and Herrath, Dv., eds, *Vitamin D: Biochemical, Chemical and Clinical Aspects Related to Calcium Metabolism*. Proceedings of the Third Workshop on Vitamin D. New York, Berlin: Walter de Gruyter, pp. 595–606.

New York City Department of City Planning (2004). Zoning Text. Available from: http://www.nyc.gov/html/dcp/html/zone/zh_resdistricts.shtml, cited June 2004.

Newton, P.W., Baum, S., Shatia, K., et al. (2001). *National 2001 State of Environment Report on Human Settlements*.

Nicklas, M.H. and Bailey, G.B. (1996). *Daylighting In Schools, Energy Costs Reduced ... Student Performance Improved*. Raleigh NC: Innovative Design.

Noonan, C. (2002). Prevalence estimates for MS in the United States and evidence of an increasing trend for women. *Neurology* 58, 136–38.

Norman, J., Kurtzke, J. and Beebe, G. (1983). Epidemiology of multiple sclerosis in the U.S. veterans: latitude, climate and risk of multiple sclerosis. *Journal of Chronic Diseases* 36, 551–59.

O'Connor, J., Lee, E., Rubinstein F. and Selkowitz, S. (1997). *Tips for Daylighting with Windows*. Lawrence Berkeley National Laboratory, LBNL Report 39945.

Okudaira, N., Kriptke, D.F. and Webster, J.B. (1983). Naturalistic studies of human light exposure. *American Journal of Physiology* 245, R613–615.

Ott, J.N. (1973). *Health and Light*. Old Greenwich CN: Devin-Adair.

Ott, J.N. (1976). Influence of fluorescent lights on hyperactivity and learning disabilities. *Journal of Learning Disabilities* 9, 417–22.

Parsons, H.M. (1974). What Happened at Hawthorn? new evidence suggests the Hawthorne effect resulted from operant reinforcement contingencies. *Science* 183, 922–32.

Porojnicu, A.C., Robsahm, T.E., Ree, A.H., et al. (2005). Season of diagnosis is a prognostic factor in Hodgkin's lymphoma: a possible role of sun-induced vitamin D. *British Journal of Cancer* 93, 571–74.

Prange, A.J., Jr, Wilson, I.C., Lynn, C.W., et al. (1974). L-tryptophan in mania: contribution to a permissive hypothesis of affective disorders. *Archives of General Psychiatry* 5, 56–62.

Parasad, G.V., Nash, M.M. and Zaltman, J.S. (2001). Seasonal variation in outpatient blood pressure in stable renal transplant recipients. *Transplantation* 72(11), 1792–94.

Rajaratnam, S.M.W. and Arendt, J. (2001). Health in a 24-h society. *The Lancet* 358(9286), 999–1005.

Reichel, H., Koeffler, H.P. and Norman, A.W. (1989). The role of vitamin D endocrine system in health and disease. *New England Journal of Medecine* 320, 980–91.

Reinhart, C.F. (2005). A simulation-based review of the ubiquitous window-head height to daylit zone depth rule-of-thumb. *Proc. 9th International*

Building Performance Simulation Association (IBPSA) Conference. Montréal, Canada, August 15–18, pp. 1011–1018.

Reiter, R.J. (1995). Oxidative processes and antioxidative defense mechanisms in the aging brain. *FASEB Journal* 9, 526–33.

Reiter, R.J. and Carneiro, R.C. (1997). Oh CS: melatonin in relation to cellular antioxidative defense mechanisms. *Hormone and Metabolic Research* 8, 363–72.

Reiter, R.J., Tan, D.X., Cabera, J., et al. (1999). The oxidant/antioxidant network: role of melatonin. *Biological Signals and Receptors* 8, 56–63.

Revicki, D.A., May, H.J. and Whitley, T.W. (1991). Reliability and validity of the work-related strain inventory among health professionals. *Behavioral Medecine* 17(3), 111–20.

Richardson, B.W. (1876). Modern sanitary science – a city of health. *Van Nostrand's Eclectic Engineering Magazine* 14, 31–42. Reprinted from *Nature* 12 (14 October 1875), 523–25 and (21 October 1875), 542–45. Available from: http://www.library.cornell.edu/Reps/DOCS/rich'son.htm, cited June 2007.

Ring, J.W. (1996). Windows, baths and solar energy in the Roman Empire. *American Journal of Archeology* 100, 717–24.

Robbins, C.L. (1986). *Daylighting: Design and Analysis*. New York: Van Nostrand Reinhold.

Robertson, K. (2005). *Daylighting Guide for Buildings*. Distributed through the Canadian Mortgage & Housing Corporation.

Romagnoli, E., et al. (1999). Hypovitaminosis D in an Italian population of healthy subjects and hospitalized patients. *British Journal of Nutrition* 81(2), 133–37.

Romm, J.J. (1999). *Cool Companies – How the Best Businesses Boost Profits and Productivity by Cutting Greenhouse Gas Emissions*. Washington DC and Covelo CA: Island Press.

Roseman, C. and Booker, J.M. (1995). Workload and environmental factors in hospital medication errors. *Nursing Research* 44(4), 226–30.

Rosenthal, N., Sack, D. and Gillin, J. (1984). Seasonal affective disorder: a description of the syndrome and preliminary findings with light therapy. *Journal of General Psychiatry* 41, 72–80.

Rostand, S.G. (1997). Ultraviolet light may contribute to geographic and racial blood pressure differences. *Hypertension* 30, 150–56.

Rudofsky, B. (1964). *Street for People: A Primer for Americans*. Garden City NY: Doubleday.

Russell, J. and Snodgrass, J. (1987). "Emotion and Environment". In Handbook of environmental psychology, D Stokols and I. Altman (eds). Ch 8, pp. 245–281. New York: Wiley.

Ruys, T. (1971). Windowless offices. *Man–Environment Systems* 1, 49–50.

Saadi, H. and Dawodu, A. (2005). Vitamin D deficiency in Arabian women and children: time for action. In: Kinger, I. and Laura, V., eds, *Trends in Lifestyle and Health Research*. Nova Science Publishers, pp. 163–74.

Saadi, H., Kazzam, E., Ghurbana, B., et al. (2006). Hypothesis: correction of low vitamin D status among Arab women will prevent heart failure and improve cardiac function in established heart failure. *European Journal of Heart Failure* 8, 694–96.

Sapse, A.T. (1997). High cortisol diseases and anti-cortisol therapy. *Pychoneuroendocrinology* 22, S3–10.

Sardar, S., Chakraborty, A. and Chatterjee, M. (1996). Comparative effectiveness of vitamin D_3 and dietary vitamin E on peroxidation of lipids and enzymes of the hepatic antioxidant system in Sprague-Dawley rats. *International Journal for Vitamin and Nutrition Research* 66, 39–45.

Saunders, J.E. (1969). The role of the level and diversity of horizontal illumination in an appraisal of a simple office task. *Lighting Research and Technology* 1, 37–46.

Savides, T.J., Messinm, S., Senger, C., et al. (1986). Natural light exposure of young adults. *Physiology and Behavior* 38, 571–74.

Scheer, F.A.J.L. and Buijs, R.M. (1999). Light affects morning cortisol in humans. *Journal of Clinical Endocrinology and Metabolism* 84, 3395–98.

Schernhammer, E.S., Laden, F., Speizer, F.E., et al. (2001). Rotating night shifts and risk of breast cancer in women participating in the nurses' health study. *Journal of the National Cancer Institute* 93, 1563–68.

Schleithoff, S.S., Zittermann, A., Stuttgen, B., et al. (2003). Low levels of intact osteocalcin in patients with congestive heart failure. *Journal of Bone and Mineral Metabolism* 21, 247–52.

Schwartz, G.G. (2005). Vitamin D and the epidemiology of prostate cancer. *Seminars in Dialysis* 18, 276–89.

Serafino, G. and Frederick, J. (1987). Global modeling of the ultraviolet solar flux incident on the biosphere. In *Assessing the Risks of Trace Gases That Can Modify the Stratosphere. EPA 400/1–87/0001H.* Washington DC: Government Printing Office, Appendix H.

Serhan, E., Newton, P., Ali, H.A., et al. (1999). Prevalence of hypovitaminosis D in Indo-Asian patients attending a rheumatology clinic. *Bone* 25(5), 609–11.

Shane, E., Mancini, D., Aaronson, K., et al. (1997). Bone mass, vitamin D deficiency, and hyperparathyroidism in congestive heart failure. *American Journal of Medecine* 103, 197–207.

Smith, H.H. (1983). *The Citizen's Guide to Zoning.* Washington DC: Planners Press; Chicago IL: Order from American Planning Association.

Sorenson, M. (2006). *Solar Power for Optimal Health.* ISBN 1-4243-1387-2.

Spaeth, D. (1985). *Mies Van Der Rohe.* London: The Architectural Press. 125 pp.

Stephan, F.K. and Zucker, I. (1972). Circadian rhythms in drinking behavior and locomotor activity of rats are eliminated by hypothalamic lesions. *Proceedings of the National Academy of Science USA* 69, 1583–86.

Stevens, R.G. (2005). Circadian disruption and breast cancer: from melatonin to clock genes. *Epidemiology* 16, 254–58.

Strauss, L. (1972). *Xenophon's Socrates.* Ithaca: Cornell University Press.

Takagi, F.G. (1977–1978). Legal protection of solar rights. *Connecticut Law Review* 10(1213), 134–39.

Tatcher, E.D. (1956). The Open rooms of the Terme del Foro at Ostia. *MAAR* 24, 169–264.

Thayer, B.M. (1995). Daylighting and productivity at Lockeed. *Solar Today* May/June, pp: 26–29.

Tummers, G.E., Janssen, P.P., Landeweerd, A., et al. (2001). A comparative study of work characteristics and reactions between general and mental health nurses: a multisample analysis. *Journal of Advanced Nursing* 36(1), 151–62.

Ulrich, R.S. (1984). View through a window may influence recovery from surgery. *Science* 224, 420–21.

United States Department of Energy (2005). *Energy Efficiency & Renewable Energy, 'Building Toolbox'.* http://www.eere.energy.gov/buildings/info/design/

Van der Rhee, H.J. and de Vries, E. (2006). Does sunlight prevent cancer? A systematic review. *European Journal of Cancer* 42, 2222–32.

Verderber, S. (1986). Dimensions of person-window transactions in the hospital environment. *Environmental Behavior* 8, 450–66.

Verderber, S. and Reuman, D. (1987). Windows, views, and health status in hospital therapeutic environments. *Journal of Architecture and Planning Research* 4, 120–33.

Waldhauser, F., Waldhauser, M., Lieberman, H.R., et al. (1984). Bioavailability of oral melatonin in humans. *Neuroendocrinology* 39, 307–13.

The Wall Street Journal (1995). 20 November.

Weaver, D.R., Stehle, J.H., Stopa, E.G., et al. (1993). Melatonin receptors in human hypothalamus and pituitary implications for circadian and reproductive responses to melatonin. *Journal of Clinical Endocrinology and Metabolism* 76, 295–301.

Webb, A.R., Pillbeam, C., Hanafin, N., et al. (1990). An evaluation of the relative contribution of exposure to sunlight and of diet to the circulating concentration of 25-hydroxyvitamin D in an elderly nursing home population in Boston. *American Journal of Clinical Nutrition* 51(6), 1075–81.

Webb, S.M. and Puig-Domingo, M. (1995). Role of melatonin in health and disease. *Clinical Endocrinology* 42, 221–34.

Weisberg, P., Scanlon, K.S., Li, R., et al. (2004). Nutritional rickets among children in the United States: review of cases reported between 1986 and 2003. *American Journal of Clinical Nutrition* 80, 1697S–1705S.

Welsh, J. (2004). Vitamin D and breast cancer: insights from animal models. *American Journal of Clinical Nutrition* 80, 1721S–24S.

Weston, H.C. (1949). *Sight, Light, and Efficiency*. London: Lewis.

Whistler, D. (1645). Disputatio medica inauguralis, de morbo puerili Anglorum, quem patrio idiomate indigenae vocant The Rickets. *Lugduni Batavorum* 1–13.

Wigmore, J.H. (1971). *Law and Justice in Tokugawa Japan 23*. New York: Kokusai Bunka Shinkokai Ed.

Wirz-Justice, A. (1998). Melatonin: new advances in sleep research and treatment. *European Neuropsychopharmacology* 8(Supplement 2), S92.

Wohlfarth, H. (1984). The effect of color-psychodynamic environmental modification on disciplinary incidents in elementary schools over one school year: a controlled study. *International Journal of Biosocial Research* 6, 38–43.

Wohlfarth, H. and Gates, K.S. (1985). The effects of color-psychodynamic environmental color and lighting modification of elementary schools on blood pressure and mood: a controlled study. *International Journal of Biosocial Research* 7, 9–16.

Wohlfarth, H. and Sam, C. (1982). The effects of color-psychodynamic environment modification upon psycho-physiological and behavioral reactions of severely handicapped children. *International Journal of Biosocial Research* 3, 10–38.

World Health Organization (1998). *Indoor Air Quality: Biological Contaminants*. Copenhagen: World Health Organization Regional Office For Europe.

Wotton, E. (1998). Daylighting codes, standards and policies. In: P*roceedings of the Daylighting '98 Conference. International Conference on Daylighting Technologies for Energy Efficiency in Building, May 11–13, Ottawa (Canada)*. pp. 271–78.

Zhdanova, I.V., Wurtman, R.J., Balcioglu, A., et al. (1998). Endogenous melatonin levels and the fate of exogenous melatonin: age effects. *Journal of Gerontology* 53A, B293–298.

Index